TOP TIPS FOR
ASPERGER STUDENTS

of related interest

Realizing the College Dream with Autism or Asperger Syndrome
A Parent's Guide to Student Success
Ann Palmer
ISBN 978 1 84310 801 6

Succeeding in College with Asperger Syndrome
A student guide
John Harpur, Maria Lawlor and Michael Fitzgerald
ISBN 978 1 84310 201 4

Freaks, Geeks and Asperger Syndrome
A User Guide to Adolescence
Luke Jackson
Foreword by Tony Attwood
ISBN 978 1 84310 098 0

TOP TIPS FOR
ASPERGER STUDENTS
How to Get the Most Out of University and College

ROSEMARY MARTIN WITH LESLIE ILIC
with a Foreword by Tas Cooper
Illustrated by Caitlin Cooper

Jessica Kingsley Publishers
London and Philadelphia

First published in 2011
by Jessica Kingsley Publishers
116 Pentonville Road
London N1 9JB, UK
and
400 Market Street, Suite 400
Philadelphia, PA 19106, USA
www.jkp.com

Copyright © Rosemary Martin 2011
Illustrations © Caitlin Cooper 2011
Foreword © Tas Cooper 2011

Library of Congress Cataloging in Publication Data
A CIP catalog record for this book is available from the Library of Congress

British Library Cataloguing in Publication Data
A CIP catalogue record for this book is available from the British Library

ISBN 978 1 84905 140 8

Printed and bound in the United States by
Thomson-Shore, 7300 Joy Road, Dexter, MI 48130

*This book is dedicated to Jonathan Tasman
Cooper, Alexander Kyle Cooper and Catherine
Beth Scudamore Cooper, with love*

Contents

About the authors

Many years ago the author, Rosemary Martin, was an undergraduate at Sussex University, in the south of England. There she met Margi Ilic, a fellow undergraduate who was an exchange student from California. After university Rosemary qualified as a lawyer and now practises law in a company; she married and had three children who are all now teenagers. The elder, Tas Cooper, was the inspiration for this book. Meanwhile, over in the States, Margi also married and had two daughters, the eldest of whom is Leslie Ilic.

When creating this book Rosemary wanted to find someone to help write the American aspects and someone to illustrate the book. Step forward Leslie Ilic who wrote the American parts and made sure the book was up to date, and Tas's friend, Caitlin Cooper (no relation), who provided the illustrations.

Leslie graduated from University of California, San Diego, with a degree in History. She lives in Southern California with too many room-mates and a dependable Volvo named Miles. Caitlin is a student based in Manchester, UK, preparing to study Illustration at university. She has been drawing ever since she could hold a pencil and hasn't looked back, her current style of drawing being somewhere between Disney and manga, both being major sources of inspiration. She enjoys rice, figure drawing and weird animals.

Acknowledgments

This book started life as a lengthy note to my elder son written in the year before he headed off to university. It developed into a book with the encouragement of Brian Cooper, the tolerance of Tas, Kyle and Beth, the help of Kathryn Horlick, and the enthusiasm and work of Leslie Ilic who edited the book from an American perspective, Caitlin Cooper who did the illustrations and Lisa Clark at Jessica Kingsley Publishers. It was a pleasure to work with each of them and I thank them for their willingness to be involved.

I compiled this book because I couldn't find a book online or in hard copy that quite fitted the bill. However, I did find numerous websites that had useful information and I have quoted extensively from those sites which I found most informative or entertaining. In particular, the realuni website (www.realuni.com) is a delight, written by and for students.

I have acknowledged each of my sources in the relevant section of the book and I set out below each of the sources from which I have taken quotes or extracts. Where I have been able to make contact with a website owner, I have sought permission to use quotes and extracts from their site.

The following sources are gratefully acknowledged:

All About Students website (www.allaboutstudents.co.uk)

BBC website (www.bbc.co.uk)

Depression Alliance website (www.depressionalliance.org)

Drugscope's website (www.drugscope.org.uk)

Durham University Finance Dept's website (www.dur.ac.uk)

Edburg, Henrick: *The Positivity Blog* (www.positivityblog.com)

Elliott, Roger: Uncommon Knowledge website (www.self-confidence.co.uk)

Financial Services Authority's website (www.fsa.org.uk)

Mindtools website (www.mindtools.com)

Netdoctor website (www.netdoctor.co.uk)

National Health Service website (www.nhs.uk/worthtalkingabout)

Realuni.com (www.realuni.com)

Royal College of Psychiatrists website (www.rpsych.ac.uk)

Segar, Mark, *A Survival Guide for People with Asperger syndrome* website (www.-users.cs.york.ac.uk)

Southampton University Student Union Guide to Freshers' Week

Stanford University website (www.stanford.edu/)

The Complete University Guide (www.thecompleteuniversityguide.co.uk)

The WebMD Website (www.webmd.com)

UCAS website (www.ucas.ac.uk)

University Students with Autism and Asperger's syndrome website (www.users.dircon.co.uk)

University at Buffalo's website (www.buffalo.edu/)

University of Melbourne's online guide: *Towards Success in Tertiary Study with Asperger's syndrome* (www.services.unimelb.edu.au/edp/downloads/aspergers.pdf)

University of New South Wales website (www.unsw.edu.au/)

US Department of Health and Human Services website (www.hhs.gov)

US Financial Literacy and Education Commission (www.mymoney.gov)

The full citations for materials referred to are set out at the end of this book.

Rosemary Martin (April 2010)

Foreword

University. One of the biggest changes you'll ever go through in your life. For some people (me at least) this loses its force after you've heard it a few times – but it's true. It doesn't need to be a scary change, though, and this guide (originally written for me) really helped me settle in.

Since I've now lived through two terms of university at the time of writing this (though it really doesn't feel like that long to me!) my mum asked me to write a foreword to this book to offer a quick overview of a first-hand perspective on the first few weeks of student life – and quite a lot of this book applies long afterwards, as well.

In the months of summer holiday between leaving school and starting university, going to university went very suddenly from seeming rather far off to extremely close. I'd been quite relaxed about it until then, but I found myself getting equally suddenly nervous about it. If you're reading this, you might well be, too. But – as clichéd as it sounds – everyone else is nervous, too. They just don't look like it. And this advice seems to get spread around a lot – later in this very same book, actually, but it bears repeating! – so people probably won't be able to tell if you're anxious as well. Or if they can, they'll probably be too busy dealing with their own nerves to care!

If your freshers' week is anything like mine, you'll end up making new friends very quickly. I expected to have loads of trouble making friends, but it was actually surprisingly easy – and I usually have very little luck with it. Within the first hour after I'd unpacked my things, I went exploring and found most of the other people in my hall milling about in the common room. One girl, sitting in a little circle with a few other people, called me over almost as soon as I came in. The expected questions were asked on all sides – what's your name, where are you from, what course are you doing, and so on – and the circle grew rather quickly into some twenty people who all looked really confident, but turned out to be just as overwhelmed by it all as I was. We got to know at least the basics about each other and some of them turned out to have much more in common with me than I'd expected – the girl who'd originally called me was even doing the exact same course as me. Just a few minutes later, we'd nicknamed our little group the 'Circle of Trust', and as more people joined us, it became the Oval of Trust and then the Random Kidney Shape of Trust. I soon found out there's nothing better than humour to draw people together! In spite of my anxiety about making friends when I arrived, we formed some remarkably quick bonds as we helped each other find our way around, and the people in that circle have been some of my best friends since.

Finding my way around for introductory things for freshers' week (and lectures for the first couple of weeks too) was quite annoying, and harder than I'd thought – university (any university!) is a *huge* place, and the university staff had, for some reason, not left the freshers' week timetable and map in my room that everyone else seemed to get. Again, I stress the importance of getting to know someone who's on the same course as you. My new friends pretty much saved my freshers' week by filling me in on things I missed until I got hold of a copy of the timetable, and giving me an impromptu tour of the campus after I missed the official one! Within a couple of weeks, despite the slight screw-up, I was very much at home at Southampton – if you somehow end up in a similar unfortunate situation, *don't let it get you down*; things improve quickly.

The highlight of freshers' week was, of course, the freshers' ball on the last day. Tickets for mine were sold out *very* quickly, and I didn't get to go to the official ball. Fortunately, there was an 'alternative freshers' ball' going on for those who didn't get tickets – it didn't have any of the headline acts of the real thing, just a student band, and nothing like as glamorous a venue (the students' union's own club instead of the town's biggest nightclub!), but it was still really fun – some of the people at the real thing said they wished they'd been at the alternative one instead! – and another excellent opportunity to make good friends and have a really fun night, despite having two left feet. It was also a useful introduction for me to that staple of university life, drinking games – expect a lot of alcohol to be going round whenever you go out!

Finding people in your hall who are doing the same course as you *really* helps. Joining clubs and societies, even if it's only a few, is also a good idea for building up a social life very easily indeed. I personally joined six clubs during freshers' week, tried them all out and quickly dropped two completely and only drop in on another two about once every couple of months – but I still made a lot of good friends from the remaining two, which I attend frequently. Parties every night during freshers' week are there for a reason. They help you feel a *lot* less nervous, though don't feel you have to go if you don't want to – I only went to a couple and the rest of the time I hid in my room. But for the equally introverted, that's what societies are there for – I was rather surprised to find out that social life at university isn't all alcohol-based! And if you *can* deal well with large parties, and can juggle more than a couple of clubs as well as work, rest and other social things – some are good at this, others like me aren't – but if you can, you'll do better than me, and I've found university to be absolutely fantastic so far.

And last of all, a couple of miscellaneous little tips. Your lecturers might expect you to call them by their first names – mine do. After so many years of calling teachers 'sir' and 'miss' this was quite a surprise, and something a part of me still isn't used to – I still quite often address emails 'Dear Professor Richards' out of habit and keep getting back 'P.S. Call me Melanie!'. It's sort of liberating, though! Also, be sure to keep in touch with your family – independence doesn't mean they won't still be there for you if you need them.

I'll leave the rest for the rest of the book. I hope you find it as useful as I did when I was first settling in, and enjoy your time at university!

Tas Cooper (April 2010)

Introduction

This book is written for young people who are heading off to college or university and who are feeling excited, but also perhaps a little unsure. It has been written for everyone but, in particular, for someone who, for whatever reason, finds some of the routines of life challenging. It aims to give you confidence, to reassure you that you can not only survive but actually enjoy your time at college. It gives you practical tips and ideas for how to manage day-to-day life. You can read it from cover to cover or you can dip into it anywhere you like.

Throughout this book I refer to 'university', but please read that as 'college' if it is a college, rather than a university, that you are heading off to. Also, it should be mentioned that not every university and college is the same. However, this guide aims to give some general guidelines, even if the specifics change slightly between different schools and different colleges.

2 The daily routine

For many students, going to university is the first time that they've lived away from home. Suddenly, the invisible props provided by a supportive family are taken away (the emotional support will still be there in the background but the support that comes from physical proximity will be gone). This means that no one will be there to make your dinner for you or remind you to grab your umbrella if it is raining. You will have to be completely responsible for yourself, which can be difficult at first. You're on your own, which can be both liberating and scary. In this chapter there are hints and tips for navigating successfully through the daily routine.

2.1 Getting up – washing, dressing, bedmaking and all that jazz

Getting up is all about making sure you step out into the day looking good, smelling good and feeling good. Here's how you do it.

2.1.1 Waking up

You will need an alarm clock to wake you, so before you go to sleep the night before remember to check that the alarm clock is on, set for the right time and that you've put it in a place where you'll be able to hear it go off. If you have trouble waking in the morning, use an alarm clock that has a 'snooze' feature – i.e. it will turn itself back on after 5–10 minutes to wake you up again. If you need the snooze feature, remember to make sure it is set to work when your alarm goes off. No point having the feature and then forgetting to use it!

Tips:

- If you find it difficult to wake up, try sleeping with the curtains open. In summer, the daylight will help to wake you.

- If you are going out the night before and won't be in a fit state to set your alarm when you get back from your evening out, set the alarm before you go out (but remember, if it is a 12-hour clock, and at 7.00 p.m. you set the alarm for 8.00, it'll go off at 8.00 p.m. not 8.00 a.m.!).

- If you have a tendency to reach out, turn the alarm off and go back to sleep, move your alarm clock out of reach so that you have to get out of bed to turn it off. Putting the alarm clock on a desk or table across the room is good, because then you have to actually get out of bed to turn it off. Once you are out of bed to turn the alarm off, it will be easy to stay up.

- When the alarm goes off, immediately after turning it off, stretch your arms and legs and open your eyes and mouth wide for a moment – to get your muscles awake.

- Don't pretend to yourself that you can wake yourself up at a certain time without an alarm clock. You might be lucky and wake naturally at the right time, but you might easily oversleep.

2.1.2 Between waking up and getting up

This can be the best part of the day. Use it well. Give yourself the luxury of a few moments before you get out of bed to:

- note any interesting dream you may have had in the night

- give thanks for a new day

- quickly run through in your mind what you are planning to do during the day.

Don't spend more than three minutes doing this – or you'll doze off again!

2.1.3 Washing

As soon as you are out of bed, throw the duvet or sheets/blanket back so that your bed airs while you are in the bathroom. Head off to the bathroom – remember to put some clothing on if you're not decently attired and you're in shared accommodation. A bathrobe works well for this because it covers everything up and it can be worn to and from the bath/shower. Also, if the floors of the communal parts of your home are a bit dodgy, put on some flip-flops or slippers to insulate your feet from the dubious things on the floor. You may want to take to the bathroom the clothes you are going to wear during the day or you may prefer to go to the bathroom in your nightwear/bathrobe and change into your day clothes when you get back to your room.

If you are in shared accommodation, it is best not to leave your washing kit in the bathroom, so remember to take it with you when you head off for your morning wash. You'll need to take:

- shampoo
- conditioner (if you use it after shampooing)
- soap (in a little plastic bag or container)
- toothbrush and toothpaste
- dental floss and mouthwash (if you use them)
- razor (if you're going to shave)
- hairbrush or comb
- deodorant
- facecloth or sponge
- your towel.

You may want to take some moisturizer with you if your skin gets dry or needs protection during the day. You may find it easier to use a shower gel which is one product that cleans hair and skin instead of lugging about separate bottles of shampoo and conditioner and soap.

Take toilet paper, too, if you can't rely on your housemates to leave supplies of it in the bathroom.

You may find it convenient to take your wash kit in a washbag, which might be a specially designed item you've bought or been given, or it could just be a plastic bag. A mesh or cloth bag is best because a plastic bag won't allow the things inside to dry, so when you use them next time they may still be moist or wet.

Take a towel if you haven't got one in the bathroom already.

Lock the bathroom door if you're in shared accommodation and then get on with your morning ablutions. People have different personal hygiene standards so everyone has his/her own routine, but here's an example of a good routine:

• First off, have a pee. Don't forget to flush the loo and put the seat down if you've raised it.

• Have a shower and wash your face, body (pay special attention to the nooks and crannies where dirt and smells can build up) and hair. Some people shower every morning, some every other day and some less frequently. It is a good idea, particularly if you are a young person (as young people tend to secrete more smells – it is part of being young!) to shower every day, just to be on the safe side.

• Dry yourself well. Put moisturizer on your face, neck and hands if you use it.

• Dry your hair with the towel and/or with a hairdryer (if there's one available) and brush or comb your hair into some semblance of order.

• Clean your teeth carefully. Some people do their teeth after breakfast – which is very sensible as it makes sure any breakfast leftovers get removed – but some like to have clean teeth before they start breakfast, in which case they'll clean them as part of the morning wash routine. Dentists recommend cleaning your teeth after meals so if you're going to keep your dentist happy, skip the pre-breakfast clean and remember to come back and clean your teeth after breakfast.

• Shave, if you're a clean-shaven male. Take care when you are doing this as a poorly shaved man can be a turn-off. Look in the mirror when you've finished to check you've shaved off the hairs in tricky places, such as on your jaw, in front of your ears, on your adam's apple and on your neck.

- Spray or roll deodorant in your armpits to keep yourself smelling fresh.

That's basically it. Put on some clothing. Check that you will be leaving the bathroom in a clean state for the next user:

- Have you left the loo in a clean state or do you need to clean it?

- Is the shower clean or have you left stray hairs in the plughole?

- Is there water on the floor that needs mopping up?

See under Chapter 12 section 12.1 on housework for how to deal with all these things.

Take all your washkit, your towel and any other belongings you don't want to leave in the bathroom and go back to your room for the next stage. It is also important to keep in mind how much time you use in the bathroom. If you have a shared bathroom, then make sure that you don't stay in too long, because your other housemates need to shower too. Also, many rooms have sinks in the room. This means that you can shower and use the toilet in the shared bathroom, and then go back to your personal room to wash your face. It is important to keep track of time, to make sure that you are not 'hogging' the bathroom, and so that you are not late to class.

2.1.4 Dressing

The key to dressing is planning. If you are not at your best first thing in the morning (and let's face it, few of us are), you can save yourself a lot of hassle by being highly organized about the dressing stage of getting up. See section 11.3 on managing your clothes for more information on clothing. For the getting dressed phase, this is what to do:

- The night before, lay out clean underwear (don't forget clean socks!) and the clothes you want to wear next day. Make sure you are choosing clothes that are appropriate for what you'll be doing and make sure they will be suitable for the weather. As you lay the clothes out, check they are clean – really look, don't just say 'yeah, they'll do' – check that the buttons are on and that the zips are working and that the clothes are clean. If anything needs ironing, iron it before you go to bed, because chances are that you'll be too rushed or your eyes won't be sufficiently open in the morning. Find the footwear you'll want and make sure it's clean.

- In the morning, get dressed carefully. Don't just throw your clothes on and get out. Make sure: your tops are on the right way round (labels should be at the back of your neck and on the inside of the clothes); your shirt tails are tucked in (if they should be); your collar is sticking out in the right places and isn't caught up in your jumper; your buttons are done up correctly and aren't skew-whiff; you've zipped up your trousers, shorts, skirt or dress; you have a belt on (if you need one) and it is done up OK; your socks match each other and are on the right way up if you're wearing them; your tights or stockings are hole-free; and your laces (if you have them on your shoes) are tied securely.

- If you wear them, put on your watch and jewellery. If you dress your hair, do that now and put on your make-up, if you wear it.

- When you're dressed, look in a mirror critically. Are you satisfied with how you look? If you bumped into the person you most admire in the street, would you feel comfortable with what you're wearing or would you wish you'd put a bit more thought and effort into it? If the former, that's great; if the latter, then you need to spruce up what you're wearing.

- Also, sometimes the weather changes from one day to the next. Look out of your window to make sure that you are dressed correctly, and have things such as an umbrella or a coat if you need one.

2.1.5 Bedmaking

Making your bed may seem like a real chore but nowadays, with the advent of duvets and comforters, it is hardly the most challenging task in the world. It is a worthwhile task – even if it is as boring as watching paint dry – because (i) it stops things getting lost amongst the bedclothes, (ii) it's a way of reminding you to think about whether the sheets need changing, (iii) you never know how the day might end and you might unexpectedly want to impress someone with a shevelled rather than dishevelled bed, and (iv) the whole place will look and feel fresher and better when the bed is made and that'll help you feel good about yourself and your environment. Also because dorm rooms are very small, it is very common to have friends sit on your bed when they are visiting your room, so if it is nicely made, it will make them feel more comfortable.

Having aired the bed while you were in the bathroom, now you can give the bottom sheet a quick tug to flatten it, put the duvet/comforter/blanket back so that it covers the bed properly and plump up your pillow. If you wear pyjamas, put them on or under the pillow so you can find them later. That's it, your bed is made and it'll be ready to welcome you back at the end of your day. See section 12.1 on housework below for information about when you need to change the bed linen. Have a quick look at the rest of your room: is it a dreadful mess or just a bit of a mess? At least once a week tidy your room: again, see section 12.1 on housework below.

2.1.6 Breakfast

Rule Number 1: do not miss breakfast. Everyone says (and everyone must be right) that breakfast is the most important meal of the day: breakfast helps you manage your weight – whether you are trying to lose weight or gain it or keep in tip-top shape – and it is important, if you want to have the energy to study well, for your mind to function properly, and to be fit for sport and other activities.

You should eat a decent breakfast, such as:

- a glass of fruit juice or water
- a bowl of cereal with semi-skimmed milk
- two slices of toast, butter/margarine and a spread
- a piece of fruit (optional but recommended)
- a cup of tea or coffee, if desired.

If you haven't left yourself time to have breakfast at home (silly you!), then you should buy something on your way into university. A cereal bar or a breakfast sandwich and a carton of fruit juice or a coffee or tea would do.

When you've finished your breakfast, as a courtesy to others who may use your kitchen, wash up your breakfast things and put away any unused food, etc. Give work surfaces and table tops a wipe with a damp cloth. If you're running out of breakfast food – milk, bread, tea/coffee, etc., – make a note to get some more and remember to take that note with you when you go to the shops. Sometimes people who live together have a system for agreeing to share communal food and drink, e.g. bread, milk, tea and coffee. If such a system operates where you live, please follow it; otherwise, you might find yourself mighty unpopular with your housemates. Some universities have dining halls or cafés that serve breakfast, which are very useful, but be sure you leave enough time to go there, buy food, and then make it to class on time (it may take more time than you think, so plan your time well).

2.1.7 Getting ready to go out in the morning

OK, so you're up, washed, dressed, breakfasted, and nearly ready to face the day. A few things yet to do, though.

First, go and clean your teeth so that your dentist stays your friend.

Next, collect together the things you need to take with you if you are going out. To make sure you've got everything you need, run through in your mind all the things you are expecting to do today. Here are some ideas for the sorts of things you need to think about:

- Do I need a coat/jacket/umbrella/boots? Do I need to take a change of clothes with me, e.g. for the gym?
- Have I got my mobile phone, and is it charged up?

- Have I got enough cash and my credit/debit card with me?

- Do I have my keys with me? Remember to keep your keys and some identification (e.g. your student ID card) with you at all times. Work out a system for remembering to take them with you whenever you go out of your room. Some people use a lanyard that they wear round their neck and on to which they attach their key and ID card; others use a small karabiner (a small metal clasp with a spring clip that climbers use) which they put their keys on and which they can clip to things to keep their keys safe. Whatever system works for you will be fine – as long as you remember to use it!

- Have I got tissues, make-up, nail file, comb/brush in my pockets/bag?

- Do I need to take a student card? A bus/rail pass? Other security/identity card?

- What am I going to do about meals today – do I need to take any food or drink with me?

- What am I doing today – have I got the books/laptop/writing paper/pens/equipment I'll need for studying? Have I got the work I need to hand in? Am I going out later and, if so, have I got the address written down and a contact phone number? Do I have my class schedule and the times of the professors' office hours and where they are located if I need them?

- Do I need to plan how I am going to get about during the day – do I need to look up train or bus times? If I've arranged to get a lift, do I know where I need to be and when? Have I got a phone number to call if I screw up the timing/arrangements?

Also, do a quick mental check to see if there is anything you need to do before you launch into the day, e.g. do you need to send an email or call someone, perhaps about a future event? Do you need to pay any bills or write to anyone and, if so, should you do that before you head out the door?

Once you are ready to leave your accommodation, do a quick check round to make sure you haven't left the iron or the cooker on, make sure windows and doors are closed and locked and generally have a quick glance round to make sure there are no mishaps waiting to happen as soon as you are out of the door. Is the milk in the fridge? Have you put away the things that you don't want anyone else who shares your accommodation to get their hands on? Once you are happy that you can leave your accommodation without it falling apart in your absence, off you go – don't forget to take your house/room key with you!

2.2 Eating lunch

It is important to maintain your health and proper nutrition is (literally) vital. Therefore you need to have three nutritionally balanced meals each day. Don't skimp on proper meals, making do with snacks instead. You won't have a well-balanced diet if you do that and you'll run the risk of becoming overweight or underweight, both of which are bad for you. It is your job to look after your body's needs. Don't forget that the way you treat your body really affects the way that you feel.

Unless a free lunch is going to be provided for you, the cheapest option is to take a lunch with you. This might be a sandwich, a drink and some fruit or a yoghurt or a cereal bar. However, if organizing your lunch first thing in the day is a bit too challenging, you can buy a meal in a cafeteria on campus or in town. If you think you will routinely be buying lunch from a café or canteen, make sure your budget allows for that cost. You may find that the university's canteens are subsidized so that meals bought there are cheaper than those bought in an ordinary café in town. It is worth looking around to see which cafés offer the best value. Sometimes universities have meal plans, where money is put on your student identity card to spend in on-campus eating places, which can be very convenient, so you don't have to carry cash. Keep in mind that at some universities the eating places on-campus will not accept your credit or debit card so you have to have cash.

2.3 And supper...

Your evening meal may be a quiet, even solitary, affair or it may be a social occasion. It can be nice to mix it up, planning your week so that some evenings you're in and other evenings you're out. Whether you are in or out, don't overlook the need to have an evening meal. This might be a simple supper or a more elaborate meal. If you are eating in – alone or entertaining others – there are some suggestions in Chapter 10 'All about food and drink' which is about easy-to-cook meals.

Tips:

• Eat three balanced meals a day.

• Making your own lunch is more economical than eating out in a café.

• The university's canteens may be subsidized and therefore cheaper than a commercial café.

• Whatever option you choose, make sure you have planned in advance, so you have a sandwich with you if you want to, or have cash on hand to buy food.

2.4 End of day routines

By starting off the day with a routine of cleaning yourself, having breakfast and preparing for the day ahead, and by ending the day with a routine of finishing off the things that have to be done that day, preparing for the next day and settling down to some good-for-you sleep, you can give yourself a kind start and end to each day which should help you feel good about yourself and the world about you. Here's how you do it.

Having navigated your way through the day, you will end up at bedtime. If you don't end up in your own bedroom, you'll need to run a slightly modified set of end-of-day routines to take account of your 'foreign' location and other distracting factors.

Again, what follows may seem like a bit of drag but, like all aspects of self-care, the time you invest in getting yourself sorted out at the end of the day and ready for the next day will be paid back many times.

At the end of the day before you dive under the bedclothes you should:

- Do your evening ablutions: at a minimum, use the toilet, wash your hands and face, and clean your teeth.

- Put any clothes that need washing into your laundry bag (if you don't have a laundry bag, use a plastic bag). If you've been to the gym, you'll need to wash your gym kit. Your underwear and T-shirt will need to be washed after they've been worn for a day. Tights or stockings need washing after each wearing, not only to keep them fresh but also to help them keep their elasticity. Your socks may last a couple of days before they need washing (but not if you're a member of the Smelly Feet Brigade!) and jeans and jumpers/other tops can probably last two or three wearings before they need washing, unless you get them particularly mucky or smelly. See also Chapter 12 'Cleanliness is next to Godliness' for more info on washing clothes, etc.

- Think about the clothes you're going to wear tomorrow. Maybe get them out and put them somewhere easy to find in the morning. Are they clean? Do they need repairing? Are your shoes/boots clean enough? If not, give them a clean now, in case you don't feel like it or haven't time in the morning (true, you probably won't feel like it in the evening either, but this is where you have to exert self-discipline!).

- Check that all your electronic gadgets – iPod, laptop, BlackBerry (or equivalent), mobile phone, camera, etc. – have fully charged batteries. If they haven't, recharge them overnight.

- Think about what you are going to do next day. This is your last chance for sorting out anything you've overlooked for the next day, e.g. that essay that needs handing in. Don't kid yourself that you'll get up early in the morning to sort it out – do it now!

- Keep things moderately clean and tidy. If you left your room in a reasonable state when you went out earlier in the day, it shouldn't need much to get it back into a reasonable state now. Don't leave your clothes in a heap on the floor, they'll become a conurbation for creepy crawlies and will get crumpled (not cool-crumpled, just dirty-looking-crumpled).

- If it is not too late in the evening, make any calls or write emails/instant messages to anyone you need to keep in contact with, e.g. your parents and other family and friends whom you may not see frequently.

3

Managing your time

Life is a whole lot easier and people tend to stay happier with you if you can organize yourself well enough to make sure you do the right things at the right time. You can save yourself a whole lot of hassle by organizing your time with the help of a schedule. Here's how you do it.

3.1 Making your schedule

It is worth saving your sanity by spending a little time each day doing some scheduling, i.e. planning how you are going to use your time: that day, that week, that term, that year. Long-term planning (the next year, the next three years) only needs to be done once in a while, say every three months or so, or whenever a big change in your life is coming down the track. Most planning needs to be about the next month, week, day, the next few hours. You can be quite loose about when and how you plan your time, but if you are a disorganized person or someone who finds time management difficult, you may find it is helpful to have a structured approach to planning how you use your time.

3.1.1 Planning a year or semester

A yearly planner which you can place on your wall or by your desk allows you to plan your work over a semester and reminds you about deadlines and upcoming commitments. The University of New South Wales has a handy year planner that you can download from http://www.lc.unsw.edu.au/onlib/time3.html. Many universities publish their own planners which also contain useful information about the university and its facilities.

- Place the planner in a position where you have easy access to it.

- Write in the dates assignments are due and exams are scheduled.

- Work out how long you will need to complete each task. Allow yourself plenty of time.

- Remember to allow for extra workload. If you have several assignments due at the same time, you will need to begin each task even earlier than usual.

- Set start dates for each task. Write them on your planner. Draw lines back from the due dates to 'start' dates. Use different colour pens for different subjects, assignments or exams. Doing this will give you a good indication of how much time you have to complete tasks and cue you to start them.

It can be very helpful to write dates down as soon as you know them. So in the first week of classes, when you receive your syllabus from each class, take a second to write them all down in your calendar. That makes it very easy to tell when you will have free time (e.g. week 2 when nothing will be due) and when you will be very busy (e.g. the last week of term when papers are due). It makes it much easier to plan events, such as a weekend home with your parents, when you know how much you will have to do the week following.

3.1.2 Shorter-term planning

During term time your daily schedule will be mainly dictated by what lectures, seminars and tutorials you need to attend and what deadlines you need to meet. Make sure you know what you have to attend and make sure you know when and where the events are happening. Work out how long it is going to take you to get to the venue and make sure you plan enough travelling time into your schedule. Avoid work congestion and unhelpful stress by planning ahead and prioritizing your studies.

You may find it helpful at the start of each week (or on a Sunday evening) to jot down in a diary, on a timetable, in an iPhone or personal organizer, or just on a piece of paper you keep with you what fixed points there are for you in the week ahead. Here's an approach you might find useful for planning each day:

- If you use a planner, then use that to schedule your day's events. If you haven't got one, you can get organized with a bit of paper and a pen. Divide the sheet of paper into five sections: morning, lunchtime, afternoon, dinner, evening. First, jot down the fixed points in your day (e.g. lectures and seminars, dates with friends, etc.), putting them into the relevant section on your planner. Make a note of where they are being held, what time they start and how long they are likely to last. Add any hours of work (if you have a part-time job). Slot in any regular sports or social commitments.

- For each event, write down how you are going to get to there and how long it is going to take you to get there.

- Make sure you have a note of any phone numbers you may need, e.g. to call to let people know if you are going to be late, or to get directions.

- Jot down other activities that you need to do but which are not at a fixed time, e.g. 'go food shopping', 'have lunch', 'hour's exercise', etc. See when you can fit these events into your day. Once again, note down where they are going to happen, how long they'll take and, again, note down how you are going to get there and how long the travelling will take.

- Now you can see how much time you have available for study. Plan time slots to use for study periods.

- Once you've got the things you have to do scheduled, you can add into your day's plan other things that you'd like to do if you have time. You should be able to see on your planner where there are gaps in your day to do these discretionary things.

Your schedule for yourself might look something like the one in Box 3.1:

Box 3.1

Monday 27 May	
0900:	Begin planning end-of-term essay today.
1015:	Bus to campus.
1100–1200:	Lecture on Romanticism. Main Lecture Theatre, Smithfield Campus.
1300:	Lunch at Maple House Canteen.
1430–1600:	Tutorial with Dr Smith (Smith's office, Floor 4, Manor House Buildings, Smithfield Campus). Hand in Keats and Romanticism essay!
1630:	Bus to supermarket. Do weekly food shop.
1800:	Do a run for exercise.
1900:	To Tina's for supper.

Get into the habit of making a written note as soon as you hear about a new deadline or new appointment. That way you're more likely to remember it – particularly if you've made a note in a diary or notebook where you'll find it again!

Tips:

- Write your schedule each week. Keep referring to it.

- Make a written note of new deadlines and appointments so that you don't forget them.

- Check your schedule each morning before you go out.

- A very helpful tool: often your university website will have a page that tells you your classes schedule each week. If you have your own printer, it is easy to print out that page each week and write other events directly onto it.

Remember: you are responsible for making – and keeping to – your schedule.

3.2 Planning your study time – and all your other activities

The University of New South Wales' website has the following valuable guidance on how to tame the time tiger. Your own university/college website may have similar information that will be specific to your campus, so take a look online. Spending time on your university website, and looking through all of the information that will be thrown at you when you first become a student, can be very helpful. It can answer many questions, as well as giving you phone numbers of people who can help if you have additional questions.

3.2.1 Plan ahead and prioritize

The first step to good time management is to prioritize your tasks. In other words, deciding which task is most important and should be completed first. For example, in a choice between reading for an essay due in four weeks or preparing a seminar presentation in two weeks, choose to prepare the presentation. It can sometimes be quite difficult to work out how best to prioritize tasks. For example, if you have six weeks to write a long essay and an exam in two weeks' time, you might think the right thing to do is to focus entirely on preparing for the exam for the next two weeks. However, if you need to order a particular book from a distant library as background reading for your long essay, you might need to prioritize ordering the book if it might take some time for it to be sent to you. Keeping up with the workload will make university seem much more manageable and fun.

3.2.2 Factors to consider when planning your time

Be flexible

Some weeks will be busier than others, and unforeseen things can happen. Remember that a timetable is only a plan or a guide. You don't have to follow it religiously every week, but try to stick to your plan as best you can. If you plan a study time slot and miss it, don't panic – look at the schedule and rearrange your time.

Be realistic

A great deal of time management is really about taking responsibility for your work. Therefore you need to be realistic about your time. Be aware of how much time you have and manage it effectively.

Be realistic about the amount of time university study and assignments will take to complete. Different tasks require different amounts of preparation time. For example, you might only need a few hours to prepare for a tutorial, but writing an assignment will take significantly longer.

You can't produce well-researched and well-written work unless you give yourself enough time to think, research and write. Brilliant assignments are not produced the night before, so start them in good time. Starting assignments early will also seriously lower your stress levels. Also, keep in mind that if you did the reading a week ago for a tutorial tomorrow, you might want to take a second to review the reading so that you are properly prepared to discuss it.

Overcommitment

Before you undertake study, you need to realistically assess all the demands on your time. Consider:

   paid employment

   family obligations

domestic duties

sport, leisure or civic commitments.

Good time management won't help if you are overcommitted. If, for example, you are a full-time student, spend more than about 12 hours per week in paid employment and spend every evening at the gym, you won't have much time left to study. If you suspect you might have taken on too much, reassess your commitments, prioritize and compromise.

3.2.3 Use time slots wisely

Students often think that they have 'no time' to study, but many of them think of study time in terms of three hours or more. Although long time slots are necessary, medium and short time slots can be used just as effectively. A well-used 15 minutes is more effective than a wasted two hours.

Different periods of time suit different activities. For example:

Short time slots

Bus and train journeys or lunch breaks are good times for this kind of work. One hour or less is useful for:

reviewing lecture notes

completing short readings

previewing long readings

doing problems

revising for exams

jotting down essay plans

proofreading an assignment.

Medium time slots

One to three hours is a good time for more concentrated study. Medium slots can be used for:

more detailed note-reviewing

reading for courses/assignments

taking notes from readings

drafting/editing an assignment

revising for exams.

Long time slots
More than three hours can be set aside for:

working on an assignment

completing an extensive amount of reading

doing research for assignments

revising for exams.

During medium and long time slots, divide study time up into one-hour sections and take breaks. Try not to study for longer than an hour at a time, as concentration begins to slip. Also remember that studying for an entire night is not effective and will not make up for neglecting to start studying earlier.

3.2.4 Tips to make study time easier

- Identify 'best time' for studying. Everyone has high and low periods of attention and concentration. Are you a 'morning person' or a 'night person'? Use your power times to study; use the down times for routines such as laundry and errands.

- Complete small tasks straight away rather than putting them off. This will encourage you to begin tackling larger tasks needing attention.

- Break difficult or 'boring' work into sections. This allows you to approach a large task as a series of manageable parts.

- Don't try to write a whole assignment in one sitting. Write it section by section.

- If you have 'writer's block', try writing something – anything – down. Even if you change it completely later, at least you've started. The alternative is having nothing at all.

- Study difficult subjects first. When you are fresh, you can process information more quickly and save time as a result.

- Use distributed learning and practice: study in shorter time blocks with short breaks between. This keeps you from getting fatigued and 'wasting time'. This type of studying is efficient because while you are taking a break, the brain is still processing the information.

- Make sure the surroundings are conducive to studying. This will allow you to reduce distractions which can 'waste time'. If there are times in the residence halls or your apartment when you know there will be noise and commotion, use that time for mindless tasks.

- Make room for entertainment and relaxation: university is more than studying. You also need to have a social life, in order to have a healthy balance in your life.

- Make sure you have time to sleep and eat properly. Sleep is often an activity (or lack of activity) that students use as their time management 'bank'. When they need a few extra hours for studying or socializing, they withdraw a few hours of sleep. Doing this makes the time they spend studying less effective because they will need a couple hours of clock time to get an hour of productive time. This is not a good way to manage yourself in relation to time.

- Try to combine activities: use the 'twofer' concept. If you are spending time at the laundry, bring your psychology notes to study. If you are waiting in line for tickets to a concert, bring your biology flashcards to memorize.

- You will only remember the information that you studied if you sleep for four or more hours that night, so don't allow yourself to spend all night studying.

Remember that it's your study and the time you spend on it is up to you. If you find yourself losing direction, sit back and think of why you are doing your degree; remembering your goals can put everything into perspective.

3.2.5 Common time wasters

Problem: Feeling so overwhelmed and anxious about your workload that you 'freeze', put things off and don't get anything done.

Solution: Get started. Actually starting a task reduces your anxiety about it. Even doing something like checking the books out of the library can make you feel as though you are accomplishing something, and make a monumental task feel more manageable.

Set priorities. List all the tasks you have to do in order of importance and urgency, and work through them one at a time.

Problem: Putting off starting a task because it feels so overwhelming or difficult that you can't face it.

Solution: Break up the workload into small chunks.

This is a very effective strategy. Break up work into as many small, achievable tasks as you can. Then when you sit down to study, you are not facing a huge, daunting pile of work, but one small task.

Complete a 'chunk' every study period. It might be a task or a period of revision. Take a break after completing a 'chunk'. If it's something you've really been dreading, reward yourself when you've done it!

Problem: Putting off starting a task because you are 'busy' with other things (even though you know you should be studying).

Solution: Feeling that you 'must' complete irrelevant tasks or do lots of 'preparation' before you can start studying is a classic procrastination tactic.

Get started. If you're anxious about a particular task, starting it can be the first step to reducing that anxiety. Don't put it off – even if you simply jot down a plan about how you will proceed further, at least you've begun.

Set study goals and vary your study techniques. Try 'chunking' your work (see above) and don't forget your reward.

Make a 'to do' list. Make a list of what you have to do in order of priority. For example, if an assignment is due next week, then it goes to the top of your 'to do' list.

Be conscious of what you're doing. If working on an assignment is at the top of your list and you catch yourself just popping out to wash the car – stop yourself and ask: 'Why am I doing this now? I'll do it after I've reached my study goal.'

Problem: Putting off starting a task because you won't be able to produce a 'perfect' result.

Solution: Instead of perfection, aim for reasonable results. Rather than aiming for a masterpiece each time, it's better to produce something – and pass – than to put it off for so long that you produce nothing at all.

If you're concerned that you won't manage to produce reasonable results, it's time to get a little help. Consult with your lecturer/tutor. Don't be afraid to ask for advice – knowing when and where to find help when you need it is part of taking control of your studies.

Problem: Daydreaming or 'drifting off' or indulging in time wasters such as computer games.
Solution: Check your energy level and concentration.

Take a short break or a little exercise every hour.

Open a window and walk around.

Make sure you are well-fed and watered – drink plenty of fluids and don't skip meals. Dehydration and low blood sugar will do nothing for your concentration.

If you drift off, try visualizing a red stop light. Hold that image for a few seconds – then switch to a green light and go back to work.

Problem: The 'Too-hard' basket: deciding that 'I didn't want to do this course/study/unit anyway!'
Solution: Students do change their minds about their studies. They may feel that they have taken the wrong path, or that their talents lie elsewhere. However, changing courses should be a rational decision, not a reaction made out of frustration because the work is 'too hard'.

Re-examine your motives for studying.

Ask for advice. Discuss difficulties with your tutor or lecturer. Seek support from student services. Don't just throw in the towel! Before making any changes, be sure about what it is you really want.

Use the 'balance sheet method':

On a piece of paper, write down all the benefits to getting item X done.

On the other side of the page, write down all the reasons you can't get it done or have been putting it off.

This activity can help you to define exactly what has been stopping you working. It's likely you'll have a list of benefits (starting with 'relief that the task is finished!') and a few reasons (such as 'I really don't understand this assignment') you can then challenge yourself to sort out.

3.2.6 Seeking help

It's easy to procrastinate when you experience difficulties with an assignment, but putting off starting only means you will have less time to work on it. If you miss an assignment deadline, you will lose marks. So, if you think you need some assistance, ask for it. Remember, good time management includes good self-management. Talk to your tutor about difficult assignments, or visit your university support services. Don't put off seeking advice – the longer you wait, the more anxious you'll feel. Most universities have excellent support systems in place to help students. Remember, there have been many undergraduates before you, and if they can do it, so can you. The university wants you to succeed, they are not trying to fail you, so most professors and lecturers will be happy to help you if you ask for assistance.

3.3 Minding the clock

Some people seem to have a built-in clock that helps them keep of track of time. They are the people who always turn up on time and always have a good grasp of what's on their schedule. Often they seem to manage to get twice as much packed into their day compared to ordinary mortals. These people are blessed. Less fortunate are the rest of humanity who came into the world without their onboard clock functionality. They have to manage their time more consciously, and that takes a bit of effort; so those poor unfortunates without an innate sense of time but with a tendency to slothfulness can really struggle to get – and keep – a handle on time management. However, it is worth the effort! Suffice it to say here that a key part of your daily routine will be to keep an eye on the time throughout the day, to make sure you are keeping to schedule. So wear a watch or keep your mobile phone's clock to hand. Wearing a watch, especially one that's set to the time of the clock at your campus, is one of the best ways to keep on schedule. It is even better than a phone because there is no risk of it ringing during class.

4 Socializing

Being sociable is one of life's greatest pleasures and can enhance your wellbeing. Some people are naturally sociable, others less so, but human beings are by nature social beings and so taking a bit of effort to get some sociability into your life is effort well spent. Almost worth getting out of bed for. Here's how you do it.

4.1 How to win friends...

Back in 1936 one of the bestsellers of all time was written: Dale Carnegie's *How to Win Friends and Influence People*. Since then, 15 million copies of the book have been sold – proof that many, many people are looking for guidance on how to make friends and socialize well.

Dale Carnegie recommended the following techniques in handling people:

- don't criticize, condemn or complain
- give honest and sincere appreciation
- arouse in the other person an eager want.

He said there are six ways to make people like you. These are:

- become genuinely interested in other people
- smile
- remember that a person's name is to him the sweetest and most important sound
- be a good listener and encourage others to talk about themselves
- talk in terms of the other person's interest, and ask questions to let them know you are interested
- make the other person feel important and do it sincerely.

Carnegie identified these twelve ways to win people round to your way of thinking:

- Avoid arguments.
- Show respect for the other person's opinions. Never tell someone they are wrong.
- If you're wrong, admit it quickly and emphatically.
- Begin in a friendly way.
- Start with questions the other person will answer 'yes' to.
- Let the other person do the talking.

- Let the other person feel the idea is his/hers.
- Try honestly to see things from the other person's point of view.
- Sympathize with the other person.
- Appeal to noble motives.
- Dramatize your ideas.
- Throw down a challenge.

He also described ways to change people without giving offence. He said:

- Begin with praise and honest appreciation.
- Call attention to other people's mistakes indirectly.
- Talk about your own mistakes first.
- Ask questions instead of directly giving orders.
- Let the other person save face (because embarrassing someone never helps the situation).
- Praise every improvement.
- Give them a fine reputation to live up to.
- Encourage them by making their faults seem easy to correct.
- Make the other person happy about doing what you suggest.

These principles remain as valid today as they were back in the 1930s. If you keep them in mind when you go into a social situation, they will be a sound bedrock for your socializing experiments.

4.2 The six main social skills

Echoing some of the principles Carnegie espoused, the 'Uncommon Knowledge' website (www.self-confidence.co.uk) describes six main social skills as follows:

1. *The ability to remain relaxed, or at a tolerable level of anxiety while in social situations* Regardless of how skilful you are in social situations, if you are too anxious, your brain is functioning in way unsuited to speaking and listening. In addition, if your body and face give the unconscious message that you are nervous, it will be more difficult to build rapport with others. You can learn techniques for relaxation. See section 7.4 on relaxation techniques below.

2. *Listening skills*, including letting others know that you are listening. There is little more attractive and seductive than being truly listened to. Good listening skills include:

   Making 'I'm listening' noises – 'Uh-huh', 'really?', 'oh yes?' etc.

   Feeding back what you've heard – 'So he went to the dentist? What happened?'

   Referring back to others' comments later on – 'You know how you were saying earlier...'

   Physical stillness, eye contact and attentiveness while the other person is talking.

   As Epictetus, the ancient Greek, said: 'Nature gave us one tongue and two ears so we could hear twice as much as we speak.'

   When you really listen to someone, they will return the favour and really listen when you speak.

3. *Empathy with and interest in others' situations* A major part of social anxiety is self-consciousness, which is

greatly alleviated by focusing strongly on someone else. A fascination (even if forced at first) with another's conversation not only increases your comfort levels, it makes them feel interesting. By asking open-ended questions – the ones that will give you more than a yes or no answer – you can have better and more fun conversations.

4. *The ability to build rapport, whether natural or learned* Rapport is a state of understanding or connection that occurs in a good social interaction. It says basically 'I am like you, we understand each other'. Rapport occurs on an unconscious level, and when it happens, the language, speech patterns, body movement and posture and other aspects of communication can synchronize down to incredibly fine levels. Rapport is an unconscious process, but it can be encouraged by conscious efforts:

   body posture 'mirroring', or movement 'matching'

   reflecting back language and speech, including rate, volume, tone and words

   feeding back what you have heard, as in (2) above.

   Neuro-linguistic programming (NLP) techniques focus on teaching you how to develop rapport. If you want to learn more about this, you might want to get hold of a NLP training book.

5. *Knowing how, when and how much to talk about yourself – 'self-disclosure'* Talking about yourself too much and too early can be a major turn-off for the other party in a conversation. Talk with people; don't 'talk at' them. A good ratio in a conversation with one other person is to listen about 60 per cent of the time and talk about 30 per cent (the remaining 10 per cent is for pauses, gaps and interruptions). Try not to talk for more than

five minutes at a time. Let the other person, or people, set the pace of the conversation. Also keep in mind what you are saying. You probably want to avoid lots of personal details when you are first meeting someone, because too much too soon will drive some people away.

Good initial small-talk is often characterized by discussion of subjects not personal to either party, or by an exchanging of personal views in a balanced way. However, as conversations and relationships progress, disclosing personal facts (small, non-emotional ones first!) leads to a feeling of getting to know each other.

6. *Appropriate eye contact* If you don't look at someone when you are talking or listening to them, they will get the idea that:

You are ignoring them.

You are untrustworthy.

You don't like the look of them (!).

This doesn't mean you have to stare at them. In fact, staring at someone while talking to them can give them the feeling that you are angry with them. Keeping your eyes on them while you are listening, of course, is only polite.

Bear in mind the following guidelines:

- To look at someone for less than one third of the time may be communicating that either you are shy (if you keep looking down) or you are dishonest (if you keep looking to the side).

- To look at someone for more than two thirds of the time may be communicating that either you like them (if you are looking at the face as a whole) or you are aggressive (if you are looking straight into their eyes).

- To look at someone for the whole time, giving steady and unbroken eye contact, can mean one of two things. Either you are challenging them (the aggressive gaze) or you fancy them (the intimate gaze). However, in other cultures (e.g. Mediterranean Europe), it can also symbolize companionship.

Of course, these are not hard-and-fast rules – eye contact, for instance, varies between cultures – but, in general, practising these will improve your social skills if you find social situations difficult. Everyone you talk to will be different, so you may have to make some adjustments to your social skills as you go. If you are having a hard time talking to someone, honesty is the best policy. Telling someone that you are a little nervous about meeting them or that the party is making you a little anxious will let them know how you feel, and will relieve some stress on your part. Usually, they will then try a little harder to find something in common to put you at ease.

4.3 Being nice is nice

People tend to like people who exude a sense of inner happiness. Where does that sense of inner happiness come from? Some people are lucky enough to be born with sunny dispositions: their glasses are always half full. Others have been blessed by excellent upbringings and happy childhoods that set them up well for life. Others are less fortunate and they have to work at gaining that sense of inner happiness. Here are some ideas from Henrik Edberg on The Positivity Blog (www.positivityblog.com) to help build that inner glow.

4.3.1. Keep a positive attitude

I am convinced that attitude is the key to success or failure in almost any of life's endeavours. Your attitude – your

perspective, your outlook, how you feel about yourself, how
you feel about other people – determines your priorities,
your actions, your values. Your attitude determines how
you interact with other people and how you interact with
yourself. (Carolyn Warner)

Constant kindness can accomplish much. As the sun makes
ice melt, kindness causes misunderstanding, mistrust and
hostility to evaporate. (Albert Schweitzer)

If your attitude is so important, then what can you do about it?
One good tip is simply to keep a positive attitude. Adopting
a positive attitude is choosing to stay positive regardless of
your external circumstances. You may not be able to do this
all the time, but being positive is a habit just like eating well
or doing your daily exercise. It can be hard to get started and
slow going at first. But when your mind gets used to this new
behaviour it becomes almost automatic. Your mind just starts
to interpret reality in a different way to how it had before.

Instead of seeing problems everywhere, it starts to zoom
in on opportunities and what's good about just about any
situation. Instead of sighing and feeling like you're working
in an uphill rut, you'll find reasons to be grateful and happy.

Yes, it might sound like wishful thinking. But it really
works. The problem is just that it is difficult to see this –
and to realize that you can actually change – from a current
worldview and attitude that may be a bit more negative.

If you'd like to read more about this, have a look at *Take*
the Positivity Challenge on the Positivity Blog for some more
reasons to change your attitude – they include making better
first impressions and becoming more attractive – and how to
do it.

4.3.2. Don't listen too much to criticism.

As Epicetus said: 'If evil be said of thee, and if it be true,
correct thyself; if it be a lie, laugh at it.' Listen to criticism.

If you feel that there is some relevance to it, explore how you can change yourself. But also recognize that sometimes people criticize you because they are not happy about their own situation. Perhaps they're having a bad day, maybe they are jealous of you or angry at someone else. Since people often are centred on themselves, it's easy to make a mistake here. Someone may criticize you, but their criticism is actually focused on something in their own life. And you are probably also focused on yourself. And therefore you draw the conclusion that the criticism must have something to do with you.

4.3.3. Treat others as you would like them to treat you

The Law of Reciprocity is strong in humans. The way in which you treat someone else will make them feel like treating you in the same way. Maybe not today or tomorrow. But over time these things have a way of evening out.

One of the most important things in relationships and conversations is your attitude. It determines a lot about your interactions and how you treat other people.

4.3.4. Use silence

Be silent, or say something better than silence. (Pythagoras)

There are several good reasons to learn to be more silent. It will help you to develop your listening skills. And instead of saying something you wish you hadn't, you can learn to keep your mouth closed. This can help you avoid unnecessary arguments and reduce the hurt you do unto others by, for example, criticizing.

Sitting in silence day in and day out while your inner pressure builds up is, of course, not good. Then you may need to speak up, take charge and change whatever it is in your environment that causes the problem. But often a great deal of negative things can be avoided just by calmly staying silent.

4.3.5. Communicate with more than your words

They may forget what you said, but they will never forget how you made them feel. (Carl W. Buechner)

I speak two languages, English and Body. (Mae West)

The words you use are just a small part of communication. How you use your tone of voice and your body language is over 90 per cent of what you are communicating.

To become a better communicator, these two areas are ridiculously important. You can, for instance, improve how you say something by loading your words with more emotions. If you have a positive attitude, you'll naturally convey more enthusiasm and positive emotions through your voice.

The attitude you have, the lens you hold up and through which you view the world determines what you see. And the thoughts you keep in your mind control how you feel. Your thoughts and feelings direct how you say something and what your hands, eyes, posture, etc. say through body language.

So even if you say nice words, you may create a different feeling in the person to whom you are talking because your thoughts, feelings, voice tonality and body language aren't aligned with your words. The attitude behind your words is absolutely crucial.

Manually correcting your body language can be useful. When you are listening, for instance, you can lean in and keep eye contact to reinforce that you are actually listening. If you keep your body language interested, you'll also be able to keep your focus and interest longer since emotions can work backwards. As your body is 'interested', your mind becomes interested and focused on what is being said.

Body language is a very intriguing aspect of communication. You can learn more about it by reading the seminal text on the subject, Desmond Morris's *Manwatching*.

4.4. Feel the fear and do it anyway

Most people feel nervous and anxious about going into a new social situation, so you're not alone if that's how you feel. Just because everyone else looks cool, confident and surrounded by friends, it probably isn't so: inside they're probably just as much a wobbling jelly as you are! Use that information to give your confidence a bit of a boost. Take a deep breath and get in there.

Try not to allow yourself to hide in your room avoiding social interaction. From time to time it is great to be able to get back to your room to chill on your own, but too much time spent on your own can make even the most self-reliant person sad and depressed. So, if necessary, force yourself to leave your room and interact with other people. If you are in halls of residence, the communal kitchen or dining room can be a good place to start.

Although it is a cliché, it is also true that joining clubs and societies can be a great way of putting yourself in a social situation in which a common area of interest can make it easier to start conversations with other members of the club or society. Students taking the same courses as you will have a shared interest in the subject you are studying, so they can be relatively easy people with whom to start up a conversation. An easy way of making conversation is by saying 'hello' to the person sitting next to you before a lecture starts. You will only have a few minutes before the lecture starts, so you can make a tiny bit of small talk, a comfortable amount when meeting someone for the first time. Remember to say 'goodbye' when the lecture is over.

Sometimes parties and clubbing environments can be quite daunting and not the easy social situations they might seem. Consuming excessive amounts of alcohol to try to make it easier will not lead to lasting or worthwhile friendships, so avoid the false friend of drink in those situations. A moderate amount of alcohol can help to relax you but watch your intake carefully: there is nothing attractive about someone who is heavily inebriated. The same goes for drug use. You lose friends very quickly when you become the one that needs help getting home or finding somewhere to vomit.

While we are on the subject of dire warnings, let me caution you against the risk of being overly generous. Generosity is a marvellous attribute, but don't let people take advantage of you. Buying rounds of drinks more often than others seem to, lending people money who don't give it back, and paying for other people's tickets and so forth can be a sign of weakness or foolishness on your part and the unscrupulous out there will take full advantage of you. Don't let them.

University life is both a dream environment for socializing and a nightmare. The first few weeks can be particularly wonderful or awful (or both!) and although it gets much easier as you get used to the way university life works, there can still be occasions throughout your time at university (and, indeed, throughout life) when events or relationships go awry. As ever, be kind to yourself if things are not going too well. Learn from your mistakes, reflect on the good bits and bad bits, remind yourself that everyone has ups and downs, put the difficulties behind you and think yourself into a positive mindset so that you can pick yourself up, brush yourself down and move on. In the first few weeks especially, meeting new people in the volumes that you will be as a new student can be very tiring. Make sure you are getting a good night's sleep, so you can make the best impression on the new people the next day.

The Southampton University Student Union gives the following advice to its new students:

- Do get to know as many people as possible. Don't just limit yourself to your flatmates. The social events organized during the first week of the academic year, Freshers' Week, are a rare chance to talk to anyone you like.

- Don't expect to get along with everyone. The point of getting to know so many people is not to be the world's most popular person. It's so you can find the ones you really get on with.

- Do join some clubs and societies. It is great fun and a good way to meet new people with similar interests.

- Don't judge a book by its cover (unless you are in the library, in which case this approach can prove essential). Your new housemate may seem a nightmare at first, but give him a chance.

- Do ask open-ended questions. People love talking about themselves, so let them talk. They'll love you for it.

- Do cook for your housemates. The quickest way to the heart is through the stomach. If you can't cook, learn – fast. At the very least, share your jaffa cakes.

- Don't forget to do your washing up. It won't just be the cleaners who hate you if you ignore it.

- Don't leave the house without a condom. The boys, the girls, the good, the bad, the ugly; everyone should be prepared.

And here are some wise observations from the University at Buffalo's website about the early days of university:

The first few weeks on campus can be a lonely period. There may be concerns about forming friendships. When new students look around, it may seem that everyone else is self-confident and socially successful. The reality is that everyone is having the same concerns.

If they allow sufficient time, students usually find peers in the university to provide structure and a valuable support system in the new environment. The important thing to remember in meeting new people is to be yourself.

Meaningful, new relationships should not be expected to develop overnight. It took a great deal of time to develop intimacy in school friendships; the same will be true of intimacy in university friendships.

Increased personal freedom can feel both wonderful and frightening. Students can come and go as they choose with no one to hassle them. At the same time, things are no longer predictable. The strange environment with new kinds of procedures and new people can create the sense of being on an emotional roller-coaster. This is normal and to be expected.

Living with housemates can present special, sometimes intense, problems. Negotiating respect of personal property, personal space, sleep, and relaxation needs can be a complex task. The complexity increases when roommates are of different ethnic/cultural backgrounds with very different values. Communicating one's legitimate needs calmly, listening with respect to a housemate's concerns, and being willing to compromise to meet each other's most important needs can promote resolution of issues.

It is unrealistic to expect that housemates will be best friends. Housemates may work out mutually satisfying living arrangements, but the reality is that each may tend to have his or her own circle of friends.

4.5 Different genuses in the species 'friend'

There are, of course, many different kinds of friend. From the people with whom you'll have a deep, lifelong supportive relationship to those passing acquaintances with whom you may happily share an interest or pass time but with whom you have no long-lasting relationship.

Friendships at university can be amongst the best you'll ever have. It is a time to keep up with friends from school/home and it is a time to broaden your circle of friends. There will be people you'll love and people you'll fall in love with. It can be a glorious time for friendships.

Online friends can be a great source of companionship. Be careful, though, to balance the amount of time you spend with online friends and the amount of time you spend with in-the-flesh friends. If you find yourself spending significantly more time communicating with your online friends than with your in-the-flesh friends, you may be missing out on the opportunity which university gives you of making close friends with the people around you.

Some so-called friends are nothing of the kind and you should keep well away from them. These are the people who are not interested in you or your welfare but are only interested in furthering their own (or some other person's) interests. These people can be manipulative and cunning. They have low morals and will not feel bad if they behave in a way that makes you feel bad or ill-at-ease. The kinds of behaviour these people indulge in can include:

- making rude or derogatory comments about other people and encouraging you to join in
- bullying or hassling other people
- asking you, directly or indirectly, to give or lend them (or other people) money or your property with no intention of repaying you
- asking you to pay for drinks, tickets or other things
- criticizing you
- laughing at you.

Often these people will seem to be genuinely friendly to begin with, but they can put more and more pressure on you. If you find that to keep a friendship going you are having to pay for a lot of things or do things with which you are not comfortable (or that you wouldn't want your family to know you are doing), then you are probably with a false-friend and you should stop seeing them. If you find they keep hassling or intimidating you, then talk to a university counsellor about it. You may need help to extricate yourself from such an unhealthy relationship.

Some friendships will be sexually charged. More on these relationships below. A common difficulty in university can be the challenge of working out which friendships are sexually based and which aren't – and, of course, friendships can change from platonic to sexual or vice versa. It can all get quite confusing.

4.6 Sexual friends

Sex is usually great but it can certainly complicate things and sometimes for some people it is not such a great experience at all. Sex is something you should only do when you're willing to do so. Never have sex if you're feeling reluctant or uncertain about it as you may find yourself feeling deeply upset about it afterwards. Don't feel pressurized into having sex if you'd rather not. Just say 'No'. Sex with the right person feels great, physically and emotionally, but sex with someone you really don't want to have sex with can feel disappointing, degrading or worse. So when it comes to sex, listen to your heart and mind carefully, they'll guide you – don't be coerced or persuaded against your will by anyone else.

The BBC website www.bbc.co.uk/switch/surgery/advice has excellent information and advice on a wide range of topics about sex and relationships including: Age of consent, Condoms, Contraception, Masturbation, Morning-after pill (emergency contraception), Oral sex, Orgasms, the Pill, Porn, Safer sex, Sex: am I ready?, Sexual intercourse, Sexually transmitted infections and Virginity. Another excellent resource, especially for American students is the Center for Disease Control Website's Sexual Health page, at www.cdc.gov/sexual health.

The BBC website also has webpages with information and advice on relationships, covering: Age: going out with older people, Age: going out with younger people, Chatting up skills, Crushes, Dumping your boyfriend/girlfriend, Exes: getting over them, Fancy: does he/she fancy you back?, Finding a girlfriend/boyfriend, Jealousy, Kissing with confidence, Love: are you in love?, Online relationships, Single: being single, and gay relationships.

The BBC website is thoroughly recommended reading. And if there is one Golden Rule to remember about sex, it is this: always use a condom.

Sexually active people have a responsibility to themselves and others to practise safe sex. Unwanted pregnancies, sexually transmitted diseases and emotional trauma resulting from bad experiences can wreak havoc in people's lives.

Being careful and acting considerately can reduce these risks. You will find there are support services at university which can give you information and advice about sex and related topics. Don't feel shy or awkward about contacting them – they are there to help you. Also, don't be shy about seeking help if you weren't as careful as you should have been, or if something happened (e.g. the condom broke). It can seem very embarrassing to go in and ask to be tested for sexually transmitted diseases, but getting them diagnosed sooner is much better than later. No amount of embarrassment should come between you and your health.

If you come to university with a sexual or long-term partner back home, you may find that your relationship is put under a great deal of strain. After all, coming to university is all about gaining independence and making new friends. You'll need to trust your partner and yourself. Talk to them about whether the emotional stress of a long-distance relationship might harm your studies. If you have serious concerns, it may be better to break the relationship before you start at university rather than part way through your course.

4.7 Notes for people on the autism spectrum

A useful book is *Making Sense of Sex: A Forthright Guide to Puberty, Sex and Relationships for People with Asperger's Syndrome*, by Sarah Attwood, which addresses just about all the issues relating to sexuality for people with AS, including helpful diagrams, explanations and practical advice. It is available from www.jkp.com.

4.8 Keeping in touch

Some of the friends you already have and some you'll make at university will last you a lifetime and bring you great pleasure. You may naturally be good at keeping in touch with your friends. If you are, then you won't need to be encouraged to remember to keep in touch with those of your friends – and your family, for that matter – who are not with you day in, day out. Social networking sites, Skype, email, even those old-fashioned media of letters, postcards and phones all make staying in touch easier than it has ever been.

4.9 In praise of courtesy

Courtesy is an old-fashioned word denoting old-fashioned values of excellence in manners, generosity of spirit and politeness. It has, to all our cost, been largely lost in today's more hurried, self-centred and brash world. Behaving with courtesy remains, though, one of the sure-fire ways to win friends and admirers. Try it, you may be pleasantly surprised by the response you get.

5

The first week at university

The first week at university can be the most exciting and the most nerve-wracking. Here's how to make the most of it.

You'll receive lots of help and guidance from the university you are joining. Read what they send you, join the Facebook and other forums that get going before you've even arrived at the university and learn the lay of the land alongside your fellow freshmen.

A really useful website about going to university is the (slightly out of date but kind-of perennial) website www.

realuni.com. It has the following description of the first week at university:

You'll probably be nervous the morning you set off to University. It's perfectly natural to be nervous, but try to enjoy it for the following reasons:

1. You're going on holiday for ten weeks, only to come home for another one at Christmas.

2. You don't have to tell your parents what you're doing.

3. You can have whoever back to your room, and make as much noise (of any sort) as you like, without your parents knowing or complaining.

4. You're going to meet loads of people with whom you will live, talk, drink, eat and sleep.

5. You are entering probably the best stage of your life so far.

5.1 The night before

> OK, the night before me and my mates went to university, we went out and got absolutely lashed… you know a final Friday before we all set off to different universities. While this was fun at the time, it didn't leave me feeling that great in the morning. In fact I was sick in the hedge, but there you go.

Not the best idea – so take it easy the night before, especially if you have a long journey!

Your university will send you directions to your accommodation. Try to work out the route before you leave in the morning. Also try to figure out how long it will take to get there. And then leave early because you don't want to be late. It's important to get there in plenty of time because the first day is when it's important to meet as many people as possible.

5.2 Arriving

If they say to arrive between 10 a.m. and 4 p.m. on the Saturday, try to get there around 11 or 12 midday, as this way you should be moved in by early afternoon, and already there should be loads of people there. You don't want to be the first and by yourself – it should already be kicking off when you get there. Arriving any later than this means you're missing out on the chance to meet people casually in the afternoon and the chance to get yourself a bit sorted. Think of it as like timing your entry to a nightclub...you want it to be fairly full, but you don't want to miss the best part of the night.

Get parent of choice to wait with car/help carry stuff up stairs (the halls will usually provide some keen students to help move heavy things) and then get everything heavy in the right place. i.e. computer on desk, kitchen stuff in corner, luggage in wardrobe, stuff on bed.

Do not stress out too much about the arrival process. It will seem like a zoo, it will be crowded with people everywhere, but if you approach the process relaxed, it will seem easy and not too chaotic. Universities do this every year; they know what they are doing even if the process doesn't seem organized. So just go with the flow and everything will be fine.

Then try to get rid of parent as quickly as possible. It can be hard for them, as it's a large turning point in their life, as well as yours.... The point where the little birdy flies from the nest, never to be seen again. Well – it's a bit different as you'll be home in a few weeks with the washing, but you know what I mean. My mum was really good – supportive and helpful, and not in a complete flap about helping me to settle in. Also keep in mind that this is a very difficult process for your parents as well. They will want to hug you, smother you with love, and probably cry, so they just need a couple of minutes of just you and them in your room before they are prepared to let go. Allow this without too much eye rolling.

When you get there, do a small bit of unpacking, i.e. enough to make your room look like a room but only quick stuff. Don't bother setting up the computer yet. Unpack the suitcase, put the bed clothes on, maybe put up a few posters, and it will seem homely in no time. You can also prop your door open during this process, which will allow people to pop their head in and introduce themselves, starting off a friendly year.

Let people know you are there. You might not do any unpacking and decide to go and talk to people. Make sure you take a shower, though! You could be quite hot and sweaty after carrying all your stuff from the car! Put on some decent clothes for the afternoon and the evening. Keep showered and looking good. You know how important first impressions are, and everyone thinks with their eyes, especially at your age.

5.3 Talk to people

Get out of your room and talk to as many people as possible. It's time to lose any inhibitions and just talk. Don't hide stuff, but don't exaggerate either. You'll be spending so much time with people, you can't pretend to be something you're not. Go round and knock on as many doors as possible. Talk to anyone and everyone because you'll be living with them for the next year. Tell everyone what room you're in and ask them to come and visit.

If there's no-one around, get on with a bit of unpacking, but let people know you're there. Set up your music system and prop the door open. This way you're getting on with something, but people will know you're there and will pop in if they pass by. Have some food ready or something, because everyone will be starving. You know, a few biscuits, some crisps – nothing fancy, but something that will be appreciated.

5.4 The first day: Saturday

Your hall and department will plan loads of activities for the first week. From the start, just go with the flow and do everything. Try not to spend a minute alone, as that's a minute wasted. Do as much as possible and loosen your inhibitions – these will be some of the best times of your life.

Normally, there will be a barbecue or something on the first evening. Let them know if you are a vegetarian, and get there early, because there will be a huge queue for food! Remember the rules about going out in the evening: don't get too drunk – it's important to make a good impression and be on your best behaviour.

Last point: whatever you do, do not miss your first day at university...

The first week at university in the UK is called Freshers' Week and is specifically designed to help you settle in to your new home and meet as many people as possible. The first week at university in the US is called Welcome Week and has many activities to make you feel at home. There is usually an 'orientation' component as well, which will help you meet lots of people in your living area (building, dorm, etc.).

Be prepared for there to be a load of forms to fill in – student cards to apply for, loans to collect, rent to pay for the first term...and take loads of passport photos with you as you'll need them for all sorts of application forms. You may find you need to take along some proof of identity, e.g. your passport or driving licence, so remember to take that with you too.

Be prepared for going out every night during the week – with a selection of events on offer. The point is that you get to know the people in your halls of residence, and also the people on your course. Try to get a mixture of both.

5.5 The second day: Sunday

A leisurely start to the day normally, with breakfast provided by most halls. You can expect to get a trip round the area, and some fun games and activities where you get out of the halls, whilst still getting to know everyone a bit better.

Expect a trip to the supermarket today as well, and realize that unless you have catered food, today you'll have start cooking for yourself. To ease the boredom and difficulties of not knowing how, why not do it in groups? Cooking with other people is a good chance to get to know them. Plus you're more likely to get a better meal out of it. Also, try to grab a few hours (maybe in the morning before everyone else gets up) to unpack the rest of your stuff. Before you leave home, have your mother show you how to cook something simple in large volumes. That way on an evening in the first week you can say 'I'm cooking _____. I would love to share if you want to make a side dish to go with it, e.g. the veggies.'

5.6 The third day: Monday

From here you'll have to start going into college to sign forms and do other silly admin things. Expect huge queues and tired feet. Use it as an opportunity, though – you get a good chance to talk to people in queues.

Other things to do today or in the week:

1. get registered with doctor and dentist

2. get student loan

3. get rent paid (if you haven't been required to do this already, well in advance of your arrival)

4. get ID cards

5. pick up any textbooks or course packets (readers) that you may need for the term, as well as school supplies.

5.7 The fourth day: Tuesday

Right, from here it's plain sailing. Expect a continuation of forms if you haven't done them already.

You'll also have to go into your department at some point for an introductory lecture and info pack, and, you guessed it, more forms to fill in. In the US, you will probably get an email giving you information about an optional information session about your major, but make sure you go!

Now you know what you're doing, so you shouldn't have too much trouble getting through the rest of the week. I'm sure it will seem like one big haze anyway!

5.8 Starting lectures

You should have your timetable by halfway through the week. It will seem like it needs its own degree to work it out, so take care and check if necessary. Make sure you don't miss the first few lectures, as they can be quite important where the professors introduce themselves and because it is the best time to meet people in the same course/major.

At the start of term, learning is the last thing on your mind. That's fine – there will be plenty of time for that later, but make sure you have all the bits and pieces you need, and keep up with the lectures. Otherwise it can be real hard to pull it back.

More on studying below, but before that let's think about body and soul.

6

Feeling good about yourself: the physical stuff

University can be best enjoyed if you are well in mind and body. Keeping physically and mentally fit takes a bit of effort, but it can – and should be – fun to get and stay in good shape (once you've got through the first few painful steps!). Here's how you do it.

6.| Have a plan

One of the joys about university life is that you are your own boss. You control how you spend your time. What you do with this freedom is your choice. You can use your time well, you can fritter it away or you can stumble along a middle path of mostly using your time well but sometimes just letting it drift by. Although a degree of slothfulness is pleasant, in the end doing nothing all the time gets pretty boring, quite depressing and can make you physically ill. To avoid these downsides, it is therefore a good idea to have a simple plan to make sure you do some physical activity from time to time in the course of a week. It is also a good idea to keep an eye on what you ingest; we are what we eat, so if we eat and drink nothing but junk, then we will be nothing but junk. Not so good. So, in your simple plan add in some items to keep your intake healthy too. Your plan might look like this:

To keep well I will:

- walk to lecture/seminars rather than catching the bus
- spend an hour doing vigorous exercise at least three times a week
- eat at least one piece of fruit or a veg once a day (yes, it should be five portions of fruit and veg a day but I can't bring myself to commit to that)
- eat junk food not more than three times a week
- eat often enough and with enough variety in my food to make sure I don't starve or get scurvy (I must remember I lose energy if I don't eat regularly enough)
- not get drunk more than once a week and never get so drunk that I fall over (and avoid drinking alcohol if I am below the legal drinking age)
- avoid drugs altogether

- go to social events at least three times a week
- call home or contact an out-of-university friend at least once every two weeks
- keep up-to-date with my studies (so I don't get too stressed)
- think of at least three life-enhancing things every morning before I leave my room
- sleep at least five hours a night.

6.2 Look after yourself physically

Keeping yourself physically healthy is an important personal responsibility. You have been given a beautiful body (even if you don't happen to like it much) and it is up to you to look after it well. You won't get another one; this one has to last you a lifetime. So be nice to it, and it will reward you with many years of trouble-free service.

There are all kinds of things that can go wrong with that complex machine, your body. Some of them are avoidable problems – avoid them if you can. Here are some things you can do:

6.2.1 Keep colds and flu at bay

Make sure you take in plenty of vitamin C (you knew that fruit was for some purpose), get enough rest, and avoid people who are coughing and sneezing. Be nice to others when you've got a cold by taking care to make sure your cold/flu germs are kept away from others. Use a paper tissue to catch your germs and wash your hands frequently to stop the germs spreading. Flu vaccinations are often readily available and cheap, if not free, on university campuses, so you may want to go get one if they are on offer (it will only hurt for a moment and it will keep you healthy for a whole season).

6.2.2 Take regular exercise

Even if you hate exercise, you have to do some; otherwise, sooner or later, bits of your body will malfunction. The minimum recommended by the US Department of Health and Human Services is as follows:

> All healthy adults need endurance exercise, which noticeably accelerates your heart rate for at least ten minutes at a time. You can get it with either moderate or vigorous exercise – you can enjoy a brisk walk, jog, dance, cycle, or swim. You can also mix it up and enjoy moderate some days and vigorous other days, if you wish.

Moderate aerobic exercise for 30 minutes a day, five days a week

How long: A minimum of 30 minutes a day. The 30 minutes can be broken up into ten-minute increments.

How often: At least five days a week.

What does moderate feel like? A moderate level of activity noticeably increases your heart rate and breathing rate. You may sweat, but you are still able to carry on a conversation.

Kinds of exercise: Brisk walking, easy jogging, treadmilling, elliptical trainer, bike riding, swimming, dancing.

What doesn't count: An easy walk of under ten minutes doesn't count as aerobic activity. You can build moderate activity into your lifestyle by walking briskly for at least ten minutes to the bus, etc. But just adding steps on your pedometer doesn't count.

Or, vigorous aerobic activity for 20 minutes on three days each week

How long: 20 minutes.

How often: At least three days a week.

What does vigorous aerobic exercise feel like? You are breathing rapidly and only able to speak in short phrases. Your heart rate is substantially increased and you are likely to be sweating.

Kinds of vigorous aerobic exercise: Running, cycling, or swimming at an intense level.

Add strength training two days a week

Moderate or vigorous aerobic activity is needed, but you also need strength training exercise two days a week.

How many: Do eight to ten strength-training exercises, eight to twelve repetitions of each exercise.

How often: Two days each week.

What are strength training exercises? Strength training exercises have you lift, push or pull to increase muscle strength and endurance. These include lifts with dumbbells and barbells. You may also use resistance bands or gym equipment.

These guidelines are the minimum for maintaining good health. If you work out for longer or more often, you further improve your fitness and reduce your risk of chronic disease and weight gain.

If you find yourself with bruises, bumps or strains as a result of exercise (or otherwise!), don't worry. Bruises, sprains and strains are very common, and usually are not very serious.

Bruises are injuries to the skin that cause the surface of the skin to turn purple, brown, or red in colour.

Strains are injuries to the muscles and tendons that result from too much or sudden stretching.

Sprains are injuries to the ligaments, the connecting tissue between bones.

Bruises, strains, and sprains should be treated with:

Rest especially for the first 24 hours

Ice put ice packs or cold gel packs on the injury for 20 minutes every four hours

Compression wrap the injured body part in an elastic bandage

Elevation for example, if you have sprained your ankle, prop your foot up on pillows to keep it at a level higher than your heart.

6.2.3 Don't sit at your computer too long

Extended periods spent sitting in front of and using a computer can cause serious long-term damage to your spine, eyesight problems and repetitive strain injury. It is essential that you take breaks. Stanford University recommends the following:

• Ensure that your computer workplace is correctly set up so that you sit properly.

• Adjust the height of your seat to allow for:

    • feet to plant comfortably on the floor (or footrest)

    • knees to bend at 90 degrees or slightly greater, and

    • thighs to rest parallel to the floor.

• Adjust seatback position to allow for:

    • hips to bend at 90 degrees or slightly greater, and

    • adequate low back support.

- Adjust seat pan depth to allow for a 5–10cm (2–4 inch) gap between the front edge of the seat and the back of your knees.
- Adjust your mouse and keyboard height to allow for:
  - hands at elbow height or slightly lower
  - forearms and hands to form straight lines, and
  - shoulders to be relaxed, with elbows hanging close to your sides.
- Adjust your monitor position to allow for:
  - the top of the screen to align at or slightly below eye level
  - straight-forward monitor viewing
  - a comfortable distance of between 40–72cm (16–28 inches), and
  - an upright head posture with chin tucked in.
- While performing daily tasks, do not exert more force than is really necessary, e.g. avoid pounding on keys while keyboarding.
- Practise developing proper postures for sitting, keyboarding, phone use, etc.
- Maintain a constant awareness of preferred neutral body postures not only at work but in all modes of your life. Your health follows you wherever you go.
- Avoid extended periods of continuous computer use by taking short breaks or performing other tasks intermittently between periods spent on the computer (maximum of 30 minutes' continuous computer use at any time).
- Take **stretch/exercise breaks** during your workday and integrate them into your daily life as well.

• Avoid direct or overly bright lighting, but make sure you have enough light to comfortably and safely do your work.

• To help relieve office stress from your body, try incorporating several of these stretching exercises into your morning warm-up and daytime work schedule. While performing these stretches do not bounce or use jerky motions nor stretch till it hurts. Do breathe deeply and relax, extend till you feel a comfortable stretch, and move smoothly and slowly.

> **Eyes** Close eyes tightly for a second, then open them widely (repeat several times).
>
> Refocus eyes momentarily on an object at least 20 feet away.
>
> **Hands** Spread fingers wide apart and hold for ten seconds, form fists for ten seconds (repeat several times).
>
> Place hands together with fingers spread apart and fingertips at chin level. Slowly lower hands, peel them apart, and reverse the process. Repeat several times.
>
> **Neck** Slowly turn head to side and hold for ten seconds. Alternate sides and repeat several times.
>
> Slowly tilt head to side and hold for 5–10 seconds. Alternate sides and repeat several times.
>
> **Shoulders** Slowly shrug shoulders in a forward circular motion. Alternate to reverse circular motion.
>
> **Low back** With hands on hips and feet about shoulder width apart, slowly lean hips forward and shoulders slightly back. Hold the stretch for 5–10 seconds.

6.2.4 Remember safe sex is happy sex

Remember all that stuff about safe sex you learnt in school? Well, it's time to use it. Make sure you know about contraception and always carry a few condoms, and make sure you learn about sexually transmitted infections. Don't be afraid to seek help from the health services at your university. They are very used to answering questions about sex, distributing condoms and performing STD tests. When it's too late, it's really too late.

Check out the following sites:

www.netdoctor.co.uk

www.nhs.uk/worthtalkingabout

www.tht.org.uk – The Terrence Higgins Trust

www.bbc.co.uk/radio1/onelife/health – Radio 1 One Life

www.webmd.com

6.2.5 Eat properly

I can't repeat this too often: eat properly. In every aspect of your university life – studying, socializing, sleeping, doing fun stuff, getting over the bad bits – you'll find it much easier and more enjoyable if you've got the right essential ingredients inside you, and not too many nor too few of them. See Chapter 8 'All about food and drink' for more info on this.

6.2.6 Don't forget to register with the doctor/ dentist

It is a good idea to register with a doctor in, or close to, your university. Many campuses have a surgery on site and the doctors in them are only too familiar with the weird and wonderful ailments that befall students. Find the practice in or near your campus and get yourself registered there. Many universities will register you automatically, especially in the US, which makes it very easy to drop in when you feel sick or have a problem. The university's website or information packets will have all you need to know about the on-campus health services. Take a note of the doctor's opening times and contact details and keep them handy in your room.

Call the health service if you:

- have a fever of 39.1°C (or 102.5°F) or higher
- have a headache accompanied by a stiff neck
- have pain with urination
- have an unusual discharge from your penis or vagina
- have a change in your menstrual cycle
- have pain in the abdomen that will not go away
- have a persistent cough, chest pain, or trouble breathing
- have pain or any other symptoms that worry you or last longer than they should.

You may be happy to continue with the dentist in your home town rather than change to one closer to university, but if you have a tendency to dodgy teeth, then it might be worth registering with a dentist close to university.

7

Feeling good about yourself: the mental stuff

Just as it is important to keep yourself in good physical shape, it is important to look after your mental health too. Mental health can be a sneaky problem. A decline in your mental health can creep up on you unobserved, gaining a strong foothold before you see it coming. As it is often more difficult to climb out of the pit of a mental health problem than it is to slide into it, it is worth taking an active approach towards maintaining a healthy mind so as to keep well away from the downwards slopes of mental health hell. Also, university is new to you, and can be stressful to begin with, so it is not uncommon for emotions to be harder to deal with. This means that whereas you may have been just a little sad at times at home, it is easy to become depressed quickly at university. The highs and lows of your mental health can seem much bigger now that you are living on your own.

7.1 Self-esteem

A key to mental wellbeing is to build your self-esteem (and keep it burnished) and to have a positive attitude. Both these can be easier said than done and you may have to unlearn some unhelpful mental habits you may have picked up during your youth as a result of having to deal with the stresses and strains of childhood. You can read more about self-esteem and how to build it by going to the Netdoctor website (www. netdoctor.co.uk/sex_relationships/facts/selfesteem.htm).

Take a look at the blog www.positivityblog.com for some ideas on how to create a positive attitude. You may find that cognitive behaviour therapy is a useful tool to help you cope well with the challenges you face. Websites such as that of the Royal College of Psychiatrists (www.rcpsych.ac.uk/ mentalhealthinfoforall/treatments/cbt.aspx) can give you more information about CBT.

7.2 Stress

You've probably already experienced a whole lot of stress during the period in which you were applying to university and doing your exams. You are unlikely to be able to escape stress altogether while you are at university – and a certain amount of stress from time to time can be OK – but you need to watch out for stress building up inside you.

There's lots of information about managing stress on the web. Here's some advice from the students on the realuni website (www.realuni.com):

> Impending deadlines and exams for courses you didn't realize existed? Ten books to read in one week? If you are going to get through it, make sure you can handle your stress and anxiety.
>
> We all get this one, and it will keep coming back time and again whenever deadlines or exams get close – even more so at university than during school days. Some people deal with it easily, whereas others can be hit really badly and it seriously affects their ability to work.
>
> It's important to realize that stress can be controlled – and you need to make sure you stay healthy. Don't spend all night working, otherwise you won't be able to concentrate on your revision, or be on the ball in your exam otherwise. Instead, arrange a proper revision schedule, and make sure you realize what you have to do, long before the deadline or exam date. There's nothing worse than feeling you haven't started early enough.

7.3 Depression

If you are under too much stress or other things are out of kilter in your life, you may find yourself becoming depressed. Don't let the depression go unattended. Depression is an illness and it can be treated. If you're depressed, the usual feelings of sadness that we all experience temporarily remain, sometimes for weeks, months and even years. They can be so intense that daily life is affected. You can't work normally, you don't want to be with your family and friends, and you stop enjoying the things you usually do.

If you're depressed, you may feel worthless, hopeless and constantly tired. In most cases, if you have mild depression, you can probably carry on but will find everyday tasks difficult. If you have severe depression, you may find your feelings so unbearable that you start thinking about suicide. About one in ten of us develops some form of depression in our lives, and one in 50 has severe depression. It affects not only those with depression, but also their families and friends.

The good news is that with the right treatment and support, most depressed people make a full recovery. It's important to seek help from your university counselling services or your doctor if you think you may be depressed.

If you're feeling suicidal or in a crisis of depression, contact your doctor as soon as possible. If you can't, or don't want to speak to your doctor about it, contact your university counselling service or call the Samaritans. You may also find these websites helpful:

www.depressionalliance.org

www.whatyoushouldknowaboutdepression.com

www.netdoctor.co.uk

7.4 Relaxation techniques

The website www.mindtools.com has lots of useful information on how to avoid stress and how to use relaxation techniques to counter stress. This section takes extracts from the Mindtools website www.mindtools.com/pages/article/newTCS_05.htm).

The following tools can all help you relax your mind and body.

7.4.I Relaxation imagery

With imagery, you substitute actual experience with scenes from your imagination. Your body reacts to these imagined scenes almost as if they were real. To relax with imagery, imagine a warm, comfortable, safe and pleasant place, and enjoy it in your imagination. Imagine a scene, place or event that you remember as safe, peaceful, restful, beautiful and happy. You can bring all your senses into the image with, for instance, sounds of running water and birds, the smell of cut grass, the taste of cool white wine, the warmth of the sun, and so on. Use the imagined place as a retreat from stress and pressure. Scenes can involve complex images such as lying on a beach in a deserted cove. You may 'see' cliffs, sea and sand around you, 'hear' the waves crashing against rocks, 'smell' the salt in the air, and 'feel' the warmth of the sun and a gentle breeze on your body. Other images might include looking at a mountain view, swimming in a tropical pool, or whatever you want. Other uses of imagery in relaxation involve creating mental pictures of stress flowing out of your body, or of stress, distractions and everyday concerns being folded away and locked into a padlocked chest.

You can also use imagery in rehearsal before a big event, allowing you to prepare for the event in your mind. Aside from allowing you to rehearse mentally, imagery also allows you to practise in advance for anything unusual that might occur, so that you are prepared and already practised in handling it. This is a technique used very commonly by top sports people, who learn good performance habits by repeatedly rehearsing performances in their imagination. When the unusual eventualities they have rehearsed using imagery occur, they have good, pre-prepared, habitual responses to them. Imagery also allows you to pre-experience achievement of your goals, helping to give you self-confidence. This is another technique used by successful athletes.

7.4.2 Deep breathing

Deep breathing is a simple but very effective method of relaxation. It is a core component of everything from the 'take ten deep breaths' approach to calming someone down, right through to yoga relaxation and meditation. It works well in conjunction with other relaxation techniques such as progressive muscular relaxation, relaxation imagery and meditation to reduce stress.

To use the technique, take a number of deep breaths and relax your body further with each breath. That's all there is to it!

7.4.3 Progressive muscular relaxation (PMR)

Progressive muscular relaxation is useful for relaxing your body when your muscles are tense. The idea behind PMR is that you tense up a group of muscles so that they are as tightly contracted as possible. Hold them in a state of extreme tension for a few seconds. Then, relax the muscles to their previous state. Finally, consciously relax the muscles even further so that you are as relaxed as possible.

By tensing your muscles first, you will probably find that you are able to relax your muscles more than would be the case if you tried to relax your muscles directly. Experiment with PMR by forming a fist, and clenching your hand as tight as you can for a few seconds. Relax your hand to its previous tension, and then consciously relax it again so that it is as loose as possible. You should feel deep relaxation in your hand muscles. For maximum relaxation, you can use PMR in conjunction with breathing techniques and imagery.

7.4.4 The 'relaxation response'

This is something that you can do for yourself by following these steps:

1. Sit quietly and comfortably.

2. Close your eyes.

3. Start by relaxing the muscles of your feet and work up your body, relaxing muscles.

4. Focus your attention on your breathing.

5. Breathe in deeply and then let your breath out. Count your breaths, and say the number of the breath as you let it out (this gives you something to do with your mind, helping you to avoid distraction).

6. Do this for ten or twenty minutes.

An even more potent alternative approach is to follow these steps, but to use relaxation imagery instead of counting breaths in step 5.

7.4.5 Meditation

Meditation is a useful and practical relaxation technique. To use it, sit in a comfortable place, close your eyes, relax your body, and focus your concentration on something for a period of time. By meditating, you rest your body, allow stress hormones to subside, and occupy your mind so that unpleasant, stressful thoughts do not intrude. Meditation is something you can learn to do yourself, or may be something you prefer to learn in classes. There is nothing mystical about meditation. On the contrary, it is something that you can do quite easily by using the relaxation response mentioned above or by using another approach such as:

1. *Focusing on an object* Here, you completely focus attention on examination of an object. Look at it in immense detail for the entire meditation. Examine the shape, colour differences, texture, temperature and movement of the object. Objects often used are flowers, candle flames or flowing designs, but you can use other objects equally effectively (e.g. alarm clocks, desk lamps or even coffee mugs!)

2. *Focusing on a sound* Some people like to focus on sounds they make. The classic example is the Sanskrit word 'Om', meaning 'perfection'. Whether or not this is practical depends on your lifestyle.

3. *Using imagery* This can be a very refreshing and pleasant way of meditating. Here, you create a mental image of a pleasant and relaxing place in your mind.

4. *Listening to meditation scripts* These can be bought online or in some health food shops and some health centres.

However you do it, it is important to keep your attention focused. If external thoughts or distractions wander into your mind, let them drift out.

7.4.6 Self-hypnosis

Self-hypnosis is when you hypnotize yourself. This is often more practical as a stress management tool than normal hypnosis, as you do not need to have a hypnotist present. The relaxation achieved with self-hypnosis can be intense. To hypnotize yourself, find somewhere comfortable and quiet, and sit down. Now, relax your body. A good way of doing this is to close your eyes and imagine waves of relaxation running down your body from your scalp downwards, washing out stress. Let the waves run in time with your breathing, first washing down over your head, then your neck, then your torso, then arms, and finally your legs. Feel the muscles in your body relaxing as the waves of relaxation wash over them. The next step is to use suggestion to deepen the state of relaxation. This can be as simple as saying something like: 'I am feeling relaxed and comfortable. With every breath I am becoming more relaxed and more comfortable…'. Alternatively, use the traditional approach of suggesting sleepiness: 'I am tired and sleepy. I can feel the heaviness in my arms and legs. I am more and more tired…'. Once you feel completely relaxed, use the relaxation suggestions.

Typical self-hypnosis sessions can last between 15 and 25 minutes; however, they can last for as long as you like.

Also, it is quite common for universities to offer relaxation/ meditation classes which are often free and a great chance to take a break from your studying and relax a bit. Check your university guides or website for information and opportunities.

7.4.7 Yoga

Working from the premise that 'Life is breath, breath is life', yoga places great emphasis on making the breathing deep, rhythmic and effective. The principle here is that essential thoughts and messages are delivered more effectively when the body is relaxed and the brain is well-oxygenated, helping the body and mind to work more successfully while feeling less tired and less stressed.

Yoga breathing lowers blood pressure and brings intense relaxation. Furthermore, improved appearance, through better posture, muscle and skin-tone, follows the dedicated practice of yoga. Bones are strengthened and joints become more flexible. And it can be amazing to see how much more flexible the body is and how much more positive one's outlook becomes with just a few months of yoga practice.

Yoga classes are readily available. You may find they're held on campus. There are various forms of yoga. The best way to get started is simply to sign up for a class and take it from there.

7.5 Anger management

Everyone feels angry from time to time. Often it is a justified and appropriate response but for some people anger can be out of proportion and can be damaging to themselves and others. That's when it becomes a problem that needs to be addressed.

Anger is a natural response, part of the mechanisms that allow humans to evolve and adapt. Anger itself isn't a bad thing, but problems occur if it isn't managed well.

When you feel angry both emotional and physical changes occur. You feel a surge of energy as adrenaline and other chemicals are released in your body. These chemicals cause physical changes to occur: your heart beats faster and you may begin to sweat and feel tense. The adrenaline can also make you more aggressive which can fuel your anger.

There are various ways to manage anger. It is a good idea to find a way that works for you, practise it, and use it whenever you feel anger welling up inside you in a potentially overwhelming way. One step-by-step approach to anger management is this:

Step 1: try to understand your own pattern of anger and where it comes from. Think about what makes you angry now and think about your life at home when you were growing up. Did members of your family get angry and lash out or did they bottle up their feelings and simmer with resentment? Were you able to voice your opinions and feelings as a child or did you feel you had to be quiet? If you are carrying with you feelings of anger, sorrow or regret from your childhood, it helps to acknowledge them and to work at changing your attitude towards these feelings. Talk about them and try to accept that nothing can change what has happened in the past. Hanging on to feelings from years gone by can cause unnecessary problems for you today. If you can identify those feelings and look at them in a new way you may be able to change the way you deal with current situations.

Step 2: look at your lifestyle and assess whether there are aspects of it that are going to lead you to being disposed to feelings of anger? A common reason for anger nowadays is stress from trying to pack too much into your life; or putting tasks and obligations to others ahead of your own needs and desires; or having money worries. Try to identify these and take action to address them. Find a pleasurable activity that will help you let off steam and prevent tension build-up and increase your self-confidence. Look after yourself physically: people who are tired or hungry or having too many processed foods in their diet can be prone to irritability and anger.

Step 3: learn to remain calm. To do this, breathe deeply from your diaphragm (just below your lungs) in long, slow breaths to give your heartbeat a chance to slow down. This breathing technique will help you feel more relaxed: sit or lie in a comfortable position, take a deep breath in, hold this and count to three, slowly breathe out, continue this until you feel more relaxed, you can then carry on with what you were doing but with a calmer frame of mind.

Step 4: learn to handle confrontation. Most people find confrontations quite difficult to deal with. You need to try to express yourself assertively without shouting or becoming agitated. Prepare what you want to say and stay calm. If you find yourself in a heated discussion, bear in mind that it is OK for people to have different opinions, try to make it clear how you feel and what you think, and be clear about what you expect to come out of the discussion. Be patient, listen to the other person, and don't take things personally. It is important to sort out disagreements with people. If you don't, anger will build up and may turn into resentment, which can cause yet more anger. If you face the situation and deal with it calmly and reasonably, you are more likely to sort it out without it developing into a serious problem.

Step 5: If anger is building up, deal with it. Don't let it simmer away up until you have a violent outburst. If possible, take yourself away from the situation and think about it. Look at the bigger picture and consider the consequences of your behaviour before you react. Ask yourself four questions about your interpretation of the situation:

- what evidence is there to show that my interpretation is correct?
- could the situation be interpreted in a different way?
- what action can I take to gain some control of the situation?
- if someone else were in this situation, what would I advise them?

Even in the heat of the moment when you get angry, you can pause to ask yourself these questions and that pause can help to break the cycle of anger. Sometimes the best thing to do is simply to walk away.

Step 6: Deal with the afterburn. There is a flip side to anger. Because of the surge of energy it creates, it can be pleasurable. This feeling is reinforced if becoming angry allows the release of feelings of frustration, or gives you a pleasurable sense of power. It's important to acknowledge this aspect of anger: it can be almost addictive. So be aware of the positive feelings you get from anger as well as the negative ones and find ways of channeling your feelings appropriately. There will be different solutions for everyone, but some strategies might include: try a non-contact competitive sport; learn relaxation or meditation; shout and scream in a private, quiet place; bang your fists into a pillow; or go running. Any of these may help to vent your frustration and burn off your negative feelings

7.6 When you need extra help

Just remember that whatever you're going through, there are people who can help, and there are many people you can talk to.

Most universities have people and facilities set aside for helping those with problems. The help is there – you just have to know where to go looking for it. You should be told when arriving at university who the best person is to talk to when you're in need – check out the Student Handbook, or the notices around halls.

- You may be able to talk to your friends and classmates about it, if it is something they may have experienced themselves.

- Talk to your parents down the phone and listen to the supportive words that come back from the other end.

- Go and talk to the university counsellor or someone who is trained to help.

7.7 When others get ill

Keep an eye out for fellow students at university who may be unwell, mentally or physically. If you think a friend may be unwell, ask them how they're feeling. You may be able to provide some support while they get help or recover. If you think someone you know is becoming increasingly anti-social and withdrawn (not just from you because they may be just avoiding you(!), but generally), then they may be suffering from depression. You may want to ask another acquaintance if they have noticed the same thing. If they have, you may want to gently ask your friend how they're feeling. If you continue to have concerns and your friend's health is declining, you may want to discuss it with a counsellor or other support staff.

7.8 Notes for people on the autistic spectrum

Marc Segar's *Coping: A Survival Guide for People with Asperger's Syndrome* suggests the following tips for people with Asperger's syndrome, but they apply equally well to anyone:

Worrying – The problem with worrying is that it will often distract you from what you need to be concentrating on if you are to solve the problem. With some problems, seeing the funny side can make it easier. If you can learn to laugh at yourself, many of your worries might go away.

Problems – Many people keep all their problems bottled up inside and look as if they're on top of the world, but, equally, many people need to talk about their problems. The trick is to talk to the right people and not the wrong ones. It is a good idea to only talk to counsellors and close family or friends about your problems; if you talk about them in public or to people whom you don't know, you may get sympathy in the short term, but you may be isolated in the long term.

Think positively, not negatively – When you do talk about your problems, try to do it without putting yourself down too much. Negative talk causes you negative feelings and negative feelings make you less able to defend yourself. You don't want to get bogged down into a vicious cycle. Try to get into a positive cycle if you can. This is called PMA (positive mental attitude), whereby thinking about your positive assets makes you feel more positive about yourself and better able to defend yourself from put-downs.

Guilt – A horrible feeling to have to deal with is guilt. If you think you are to blame for something, you must ask yourself if you knew that you were doing something wrong. If you didn't know, or you only had a vague feeling about it, then you cannot blame yourself, even if other people are. All you can do is to tell yourself that you'll try not to do it again.

Often apologizing to someone can help to ease the guilt and improve your relationship with that person.

You can do it Remember, the key word is determination and if you know in your heart you can do something, then you must go for it.

The University of Melbourne's online guide, *Towards Success in Tertiary Study with Asperger's Syndrome*, also has some useful advice for students with Asperger's, as follows:

Students need to learn how to recognize stress factors and manage stress levels. Stress factors may include:

Less flexible timelines or assessment

Dissatisfaction with assignments or essays

Negative feedback or low marks

Unexpected changes such as cancelled, rescheduled or relocated classes

Pace of course

Absenteeism

Unpleasant or uninteresting topics

Social interaction.

Some suggestions for managing stress include:

Talk to a counsellor about triggers and management techniques.

Find a space on campus to use as a quiet retreat.

Practise most effective relaxation techniques.

Develop and practise social skills and managing personal interactions.

Cultivate friendships: join clubs and study groups and online discussion lists.

8 Money matters

Money matters. You probably won't have much of it while you're a student so you'll need to get used to managing on a tight budget (unless you want to run up a huge debt which really isn't a great idea). Here are some ways of getting by financially.

8.1 Budgeting

Have a look at the budgeting section of the UCAS website for a helpful introduction to student finances (www.ucas.com/students/startinguni/managing_money/budgeting/).

The following advice comes from www.thecompleteuniversity guide.co.uk.

If you have not already done so, estimate your annual budget by listing all your expected income, including any savings you will bring with you to university. See how this compares with your anticipated expenditure in the hope that the balance sheet almost balances or, better still, that you are left with spare cash in the bank for doing what you've always wanted to do!

However, budgeting accurately is never an easy process. It can be difficult to predict accurately some variable expenses such as entertainment. Start by identifying bills which must be paid and include in this a small contingency fund. This will leave you with the 'flexible' part of your income to take weekly from the bank. Don't be too optimistic in your first budget, and do be aware of how much you actually spend (try writing down *everything* you spend over a week or so). Budget for university gigs and balls, birthdays and parties, or you may find yourself missing out on the best social events of the year. If there is a big gap between planned budget and actual expenditure, perhaps your spending habits need attention rather than your budgeting. Above all, remember to keep a check on your finances so that money worries do not detract from your studying and from enjoying university life. Clearly, your patterns of expenditure will differ significantly between term-time and vacations and you will need to allow for this.

8.2.1 Money survival tips for students in the United Kingdom

Take out your maximum student loans, if only to invest some of it elsewhere.

Check what grants and bursaries are available to you.

Sign on with the bank which offers the best long-term benefits.

Find a part-time job and be paid gross if you are not liable for tax.

Make the most of any student discounts.

Get to know how to use the library at the earliest opportunity.

Use the internet to buy and sell on secure sites.

Opt for the best value telephone landline provider.

Keep an eye open for the best mobile package.

Buy essential books and equipment second-hand.

Shop in local markets, charity shops and the students' union.

Be careful with heating and lighting.

Try and buy in bulk if living in a student house.

Share to save whenever you can, particularly on transport.

Walk or cycle during the day rather than take public transport.

Check to see if your belongings can be covered by your family insurance.

Try drawing up a weekly budget and sticking to it.

8.2.2 Money survival tips for students in the United States

Check what scholarships are available, and check online to see what student aid you have received from the school, if any.

Keep track of your school meal plan, to make sure you are not overspending, and that the plan will last the whole year.

Avoid buying things in the over-priced on-campus stores; go off campus instead.

Get a bus pass from your campus; they will be free or very reduced.

Use Amazon and other websites to buy your textbooks, because the prices are much lower.

Check out part-time student jobs, which are readily available on campus and very convenient.

If you are living off campus, make sure you are using energy efficiently, by turning off lights and such when you leave.

Find the grocery store with the best deals, which is probably not the one closest to campus.

Check out the campus box office; they often have reduced ticket prices for movie theatres and nearby attractions.

8.3 Example budget

You can use the Budget Planner at the back of this book to plan your own budget. The example below, taken from Durham University Finance Department's website, is a bit out of date (2007 costs), so if you want to tailor the example to your own budget, remember to update the costs. For American students, the form is still valid, just fill everything in with the dollar amounts.

Katie is 18 years old. She is starting a degree in October. She will be living in college accommodation during her first year. Katie wants to make the most out of her time at Durham, and get involved with some extra-curricular activities if she can. She hopes not to have to get a part-time job in term-time so she can concentrate on university life, but has arranged three weeks' paid work in her Christmas and Easter vacations at the supermarket where she worked throughout her sixth form. Katie's household income is £25,000.

One academic year (38 weeks)
Step one: income

INCOME	£ OVER THE ACADEMIC YEAR
Statutory Support for Tuition Fees	
Tuition Fee Loan	£3,000
Statutory Support for Living and Other Course Costs	
Maintenance Grant	£1,450
Maintenance Loan	£3,205
Durham Grant	£1,500
Unearned Income	
Family Contributions to Tuition Fees	£0
Family Contributions to Living and other Course Costs	£0
Interest-free Bank Overdraft	£1,000
Earned Income	
Income from Part-time Work during Term-time	£0
Income from Vacation Work	£510
Savings	£250
Partner's Earnings	£0
Statutory Support for Extra Costs	
Special Support Grant	£0
Adult Dependants Grant	£0
Childcare Grant	£0
Parents Learning Allowance	£0
Disabled Students Allowance	£0
Tax Credits	
Child Tax Credit	£0
Working Tax Credit	£0

Benefits	
Child Benefit	£0
Income Support	£0
Housing Benefit	£0
Other	
Money from Grandma	£500
Total	**£11,415**

Step two: necessary expenditure

EXPENDITURE	£ OVER THE ACADEMIC YEAR
Tuition Fees	£3,000
College Accommodation	£3,945
Laundry Costs	£70
Rent	£0
Mortgage and Buildings Insurance	£0
Council Tax	£0
Contents Insurance	£60
Utilities (Water, Gas, Electricity, Oil or Solid Fuel)	£0
Landline (Line Rental ONLY, not call costs)	£0
Food and Household Shopping	£0
Travel (Train Tickets between Home and University)	£150
Toiletries	£190
Childcare	£0
Course Costs (e.g. stationery, books, laboratory equipment, field trips, NOT Tuition Fees)	£300
Minimum Debt Repayments	£0
Partner's Essential Expenditure	£0
Total	£7,655

Step three: difference between income and expenditure

	£ OVER THE ACADEMIC YEAR
My Income	£11,415
My Necessary Expenditure	£7,655
Difference	£3,760

Step four: luxury expenditure

LUXURY EXPENDITURE	£ OVER THE ACADEMIC YEAR
Clothing *(I probably won't need too many new clothes, just new shoes if the old ones wear out, the odd cheap outfit if I'm going out, that kind of thing).*	£250
Leisure *(I'm going to allow £25 per week)*	£950
Landline (Call Costs ONLY)	£0
Mobile Phone *(I'm going to allow £5 per week)*	£190
Christmas and Birthday Presents *(I'm going to pay for these out of my vacation earnings)*	£100
Extra-Curricular Activities *(I'm not sure how much it will cost to do the things I want to do, so I'm going to budget a lot and if it doesn't cost that much I can always change my budget)*	£250
Treats *(I might want a treat to cheer me up or celebrate or something now and then during the academic year, so I'll budget for allowing myself some treats. I'm going to pay for my treats out of my vacation earnings)*	£150
Travel During the Long Vacation *(I'm really hoping to go interrailing during the Long Vacation)*	£1,000
Total	**£2,740**

Step five: total income and expenditure

	£ OVER THE ACADEMIC YEAR
My Income	*£11,415*
My Total Expenditure	*£10,395*
Difference	**£1,020**

According to my budget I'll have £1,020 left over at the end of the academic year. I'm going to leave my budget like it is though, in case I have any unexpected costs or emergencies during the academic year.

8.4 Managing cash flow

Managing your cash flow through the academic year is an important part of budgeting. There may be points in the year, especially before the start of each term or when your residence charge/rent is debited from your account, when you'll need to be extra careful with your expenditure.

For any periods of the year where you may have less money than required (e.g. just before your maintenance loan/grant is paid to you) to meet direct debits or other essential payments you may want to consider an interest free overdraft from your student bank account to avoid penalty charges.

8.5 Opening and running a bank account

There is plenty of choice for students opening bank accounts, so it pays to shop around and look for the most student-friendly deal. The price comparison websites, such as www.moneysupermarket.com, can be good places to start the search. In particular, check out the annual percentage rate (APR) of interest on monies you borrow from the bank.

Although the banks try to make opening a bank account relatively easy, it can still be a bit of a hassle as you have to prove you are who you say you are.

You may wish to switch accounts if you're moving home, or to get a better deal. Check the interest rate and overdraft charges to see if you'd be better off. Some banks offer an automatic switching service when you move your account to them, by arranging to contact your employer if you have one (for your pay), and any regular payments that you have set up, to move them over.

Make sure the bank account has what you need, not only a current account but also, for example, a credit card, a debit card, an overdraft facility, a loan facility, internet and phone banking.

Once your account is open, make sure you check the balance in your account frequently – at least once a week. You need to know how fast you are spending your money and how much you have left.

If you have money or cheques to pay into your bank account, try to pay them in promptly; otherwise you may lose them. When you want to withdraw money from your account, you can use a debit card in a 'hole in the wall' machine (ATM) or you can draw money out by handing a completed cheque, made payable to yourself, to a bank teller (the bank employee sitting behind a counter).

Try to avoid using a credit card if possible, as you can incur a lot of interest on the amount you owe on the card. A credit card is a form of borrowing. You have a limit up to which you can spend. Almost all credit cards give you some period of interest-free credit for purchases, as long as the bill is paid in full every month by the payment date. This interest-free period can vary between credit cards. If you do use a credit card, try to pay off the full amount outstanding on the card each month. That way, you can avoid paying interest charges.

The Financial Services Authority provides the following advice on running a bank account, and for students in the United States, information specific to the US can be found at the US Financial Literacy and Education Commission (www.mymoney.gov).

You can use your bank account to pay money in and out in various ways. Here are some tips on how to keep track of your money.

Usually there are three stages:

1. Paying (putting) money in

    -   You can take cash and cheques made payable to you to your local bank branch, and complete a paying-in form.

    -   You can pay in cheques made payable to you, by post to your branch.

    -   Your bank account can receive automated transfers, such as your salary, paid straight into your account by your employer. This is known as payment by BACS and your employer will need your bank details to do this, including your sort code and your account number. You'll find these on your bank statement, cheque book or card.

    -   Keep your bank details safe and protect yourself against fraud.

2. Paying (taking) money out

    -   Get cash out from a cash machine or ATM, at the supermarket and other shops (known as cashback), or at your branch. There is a limit to how much you can get each time. This money is deducted from your account straight away.

    -   Pay for goods using your debit card or by cheque. This usually takes between three to five working days, so check with your bank.

- Pay bills by direct debit, standing order, cheque, telephone or online banking. Some banks are now using the Faster Payments Service (FPS) for internet, phone or standing order payments. This means that payment can be made on the same day for standing orders and within two hours for phone or internet payments. Your bank will tell you when your account is enabled to use the FPS. You can check that the receiving account is allowed to receive faster payments by asking your bank or using the APACS sort-code checker.

For information about using cheques safely, paying safely online and an explanation of what happens when you pay by debit card, visit the APACS website.

In the UK, we now use 'chip and PIN' for the vast majority of our transactions. Chip and PIN means your cards are better protected from fraud. In the US, we use PI cards which means they swipe the card like a regular credit card but require a PIN to access it, which also prevents fraud.

Make sure you keep track of how much money is left in your account, because if you go overdrawn (which will happen if you take more money out of your account than is actually in it) you may be charged.

3. Keeping track of your money

  - Check statements from your bank and report anything wrong.

  - Check receipts or mini-statements from cash machines and report anything wrong.

  - Fill in cheque book stubs to keep track of what cheques you have written and who you've written them to.

- Keep paying-in stubs until the money has arrived in your account.

- Keep track of where your money is going and keep your bank statements in a safe place. You may need them for tax purposes.

- It's a good idea to shred any personal data once you no longer need to keep it – this helps protect you against identity fraud.

8.6 Savings and investments

You will probably find you can't save much (or any!) money while you are a student. If, however, you do find that money is building up in your current account, you should look into opening a savings account so that you can earn some interest on the money you've got. There are many different ways of saving money. If you are unsure what is suitable for you, take a look at the Financial Services Authority's website (www.moneymadeclear.org.uk/hubs/home_savings.html) for an introduction to the various kinds of savings account available.

8.7 Debt

If you use an overdraft facility or take out a loan, you are incurring debt. Debt can be difficult to manage and some people find themselves getting into difficulties when they find they can't repay the debt. Before you take on debt, make sure you know what you are getting into. The Financial Services Authority has a simple guide about debt, including a handy jargon-buster (www.moneymadeclear.org).

As the UCAS website says, it is easy to spend money quickly, but if you get into debt, it's usually much harder to pay it off. A debt created from an overdraft or credit card can take months or even years to pay off, so imagine what it would be like if you have built up debts on an overdraft, loan, and from a credit card and half a dozen store cards.

With careful budgeting, you can avoid this trap by planning your spending – that way you know your incomings, outgoings and how much you have left to play with, so you are never caught off-guard with a huge bill that you can't pay. If you do run into problems, try to economize – work out what you can live without or what you can cut back on so that you make savings and avoid getting into too much debt. Many people believe that taking out yet another loan to pay off previous debts will help, but this can make matters worse as you could end up paying more interest on the new loan.

The best way to tackle debt is to set up a payment plan: put in a realistic amount each week or month and work out how long it will take to pay it off. This way, you can avoid the stress of debt, and focus on studying.

For free confidential advice about how to deal with debt problems, you can use the National Debtline website, www. nationaldebtline.co.uk or contact the Citizens Advice Bureau, www.citizensadvice.co.uk. Also most universities have Student Money Advisers or other student support staff who can help with questions or problems about money. Students in the US can check out the advice of the Federal Trade Commission at http://ftc.gov/bcp/edu/pubs/consumer/credit/cre13.shtm.

8.8 Student discount cards (for the United Kingdom)

Holders of National Union of Students (NUS) cards can claim discounts at lots of places. And a 16–25 Railcard also offers valuable savings, which you can also get if you're over 25 and still in full-time education. Check with your university, college or local bus company as many areas offer special travel cards for students and some universities may offer free student bus services. You may also be able to get a discount on your TV licence if you go home for the summer, so find out how.

8.9 How to manage your finances day to day

It is an obvious point, but it is a good idea to check before you go out in the morning that you've got some cash on you and your debit card. If you can see that you are going to run out of cash during the day make sure you build in time to get to an ATM or bank to replenish your cash. If you can't find an ATM or bank nearby, you may be able to get cash at a supermarket by using the 'cashback' facility that many of them provide. You'll need to buy something at the supermarket (some supermarkets require you to spend over a certain amount, e.g. £10, before they'll provide the cashback service) and then when you come to pay for what you've bought use your debit card and ask the till operator if you can have cashback. They'll ask how much you want (there is usually an upper limit of £50) and then they will add that amount to your debit card and give you the cash.

Monitor the balance in your current account regularly. It can go down to nothing surprisingly quickly. If you can, you should avoid being overdrawn on your current account as you will find that the bank may charge you high overdraft fees for being overdrawn. If you think you are likely to become overdrawn, contact your bank before you become overdrawn and ask if you can arrange an overdraft facility. Most student bank accounts come with an automatic overdraft facility – make sure you are aware of what the arrangement is before you need it. However, in the US overdraft facilities are rare, which means that banks will be very unhappy with you if you take out more money than you have, and you will have to pay them back as well as being charged large fees.

8.10 Insurance for students

You need to get your stuff insured while you are at university. Students' stuff can cost in the region of £5,000 – it is worth insuring that much value. Your parents' home insurance policy probably won't cover your stuff at university so you'll need to look around and secure yourself some suitable insurance. In the UK Endsleigh is a well-known provider of insurance for students but there are plenty of competing offers so look around before you buy. The All About Students website (www.allaboutstudents.co.uk) has some useful comparison information.

Don't forget that you might need to take out additional insurance to cover special things, such as electronics, musical instruments and so forth. Also, you may want to get travel insurance, and some students may want to get life insurance cover, too.

Students in the United States should check about the insurance levels with the school, but usually the dorms will provide some insurance. School will also have the best information about who to go for to get insurance if you would like to buy additional coverage.

8.11 Tax

8.11.1 Know where you stand when it comes to tax in the United Kingdom

Your tax position as a student is that any grant is non-taxable. In general, so are any scholarships, bursaries, research awards and housing benefit you might get. In other words, you can get any or all of these and still keep your full tax allowances.

Everyone can earn or receive an amount of income in each tax year before paying tax. This is called the personal allowance. If your income is below that in the tax year, you won't have to pay any tax (a tax year starts on 6 April in one year and finishes on 5 April in the next).

You can find out more about your liability to pay tax on the HMRC website, see www.hmrc.gov.uk/students/faqs.htm for Frequently Asked Questions about student's tax.

8.11.2 Know where you stand when it comes to tax in the United States

Students only have to file income taxes if they are working. If you do work, make sure to file taxes before April, and to keep track of where your W2s and other important documents are going. It is quite common to list your parents' home as a permanent address when you are applying for jobs, so keep track and make sure you get the documents from your parents' house when it's time to file. If you are a student who is not working, then you probably won't have to file taxes, unless you are getting special grants, because you will still be considered a dependent on your parents' taxes. More information can be found at www.irs.gov.

9

Getting a job while at university

Many students want and/or need to find part-time and vacation jobs. Fortunately, there are plenty of ways of finding work suitable for students, even if there isn't always a surfeit of actual jobs available. Your university students' union may run a database of temporary and part-time job opportunities near your university, and that can be an ideal place to check for jobs. There are plenty of online student job search websites, too, such as www.e4s.co.uk and www.student-jobs.co.uk. USAJobs.gov is a great resource for students in the United States, especially for entry-level positions.

You can also use the Job Centre Plus service, employment agencies and classified adverts in newspapers and online.

Some examples of student jobs include administration, information technology, bar work, waiting on tables, telemarketing, market research, retail and driving.

If you work for a large company, you may also find the added benefit of being able to work for them in your home town during the holidays or vice versa.

The largest single area of employment is retail, where there is more demand for flexible part-time workers. Although it might be tempting to take on lots of shifts, there's no point getting extra cash if it ruins your chances of studying. You need to get the balance right, so don't burn yourself out. If you do work while studying, check that your employer meets their legal obligations to you – conditions of service and health and safety provision.

It is very important to make sure you still have time to study. It is best to wait until you have adjusted to student life, perhaps halfway through your first term, to take on a job. Signing up for a job in the first week may cause problems, because as the term goes on you may not have as much time to work as you originally thought you did. By taking a job later, you can give your employer definite estimates about how often you will be available to work.

All about food and drink

Preparing meals can be a lot of fun, particularly if it is a team effort (although it can end in tears, too, if there are too many cooks in the kitchen). Lots of students, though, steer clear of actually cooking anything and get by on a curious diet of often rather unhealthy foods. This section gives you some of the basics about cooking and food hygiene and gives you some ideas for recipes.

10.1 Stock up your larder

It's useful to keep certain items handy at all times, because they're used in many different types of recipes. With these basic ingredients, you can pretty much knock something up any time you are hungry.

Oil (vegetable, olive, sunflower, etc.)

Herbs and spices: garlic, basil, parsley, oregano, chilli, paprika, cumin, coriander, turmeric, etc. etc. Get more if you cook more. Dried is fine. Pesto is handy. However, don't feel that you have to have all of these; just bring the ones you commonly use at home.

Salt and pepper

Flour (plain and bread flour)

Sugar

Pasta (spaghetti is by far the cheapest type of pasta)

Potatoes

Rice (the bigger the bag, the cheaper per kg/lb)

Tins of beans, tomatoes, more beans, spaghetti

Cheese of some variety

Instant food such as Uncle Ben's two-minute rice or the powdered soup that just requires water

Ketchup and any other sauces you like such as salad cream or mayonnaise.

10.2 Preparing meals

There are lots of websites with recipes for students. Check out, for example, www.thestudentroom.co.uk/wiki/Student_Food and www.studentrecipes.com.

Pasta

As our friends on the realuni website say: know how to cook pasta, and you're sorted.

It goes something like this:

1. Turn on the cooker hob to max (student cookers are either on or off – there will be no temperature control, so don't even think about trying...).
2. Boil kettle, because this is quicker than heating the water on the hob. Fill a saucepan at least half full of boiling water.
3. Add pasta – normally a mugfull is enough for one person. Yes, I know it doesn't look like much, but it expands.
4. Cook for about ten minutes, until squidgy and nice tasting.
5. Don't burn your tongue when trying it!
6. Use a colander to strain off the water, or you'll dump it all in the sink.

What to have with it

Here is where you can use your individuality.... Try these:

1. tomato stuff from a jar and tuna (real quick)
2. tomato stuff from a jar and chopped sausage that you've fried

For a real change:

1. tomato stuff from a jar and bacon
2. plain grated cheese
3. tuna and a tin of sweetcorn
4. meatballs, bought frozen and heated in the oven or microwave

5. cheese and ketchup

6. warmed olive oil with crushed garlic and cheese

7. pesto, stirred into the drained pasta and briefly heated in the saucepan

8. bacon bits and cheese

9. bought pasta sauce, stirred into the drained pasta and briefly heated in the saucepan

10. fried chicken breast, bacon and onion with some broccoli, carrots and soy sauce.

The observant of you will have realized pasta and tomato is a common theme amongst students. Another common theme is a distinct lack of vegetables…

Vegetables that can be eaten without cooking:

1. carrots, cut into strips if you want them to look pretty

2. celery

3. red or yellow peppers, cut into strips with all the seeds removed

4. tins of sweetcorn (directly eaten from the can with a spoon is OK)

5. cucumber

6. lettuce, nice with a bit of dressing

7. baby tomatoes

8. broccoli, well cleaned and cut into little bunches

9. green beans, or pretty much any other vegetable, straight out of a can

10. snow peas, or edible pod peas.

SORT IT OUT – YOU'RE SUPPOSED TO HAVE FIVE PORTIONS OF FRUIT AND VEG A DAY – and a tin of baked beans counts as 1!

10.3 Eating out

Eating out can be a mimimalist snack-on-the-run to a maximilist full-blown banquet with friends and anything in-between. If you are planning to eat out with friends, you'll need to check out the prices of various restaurants and choose one that fits your budget. You may need to book a table at a restaurant that is popular or on a popular night for eating out, e.g. Saturday.

Another option is dining with a group in one of the university's dining halls or canteens. This may feel like going out to dinner, especially when done with a lot of friends, but it won't take too much out of your wallet.

When you eat at a restaurant that has waiter service, you should expect to leave the waiter a tip of an amount equal to about 10 per cent of the meal bill.

10.4 Know your limits

Although alcohol consumption is a popular pastime for many students, it does have some disadvantages (it's expensive, rots your brain cells, can lead to addiction problems if taken to excess, can make you unpleasantly drunk – unpleasant for yourself and possibly others – and so on). So know what your limits are when it comes to alcohol consumption. And *never* drive when you are over the legal alcohol limit. The safest thing to do if you are planning to drive home after an evening out is not to drink alcohol at all during the evening; that way you won't be at risk of being inadvertently over the limit.

Also, drinking when you are underage (18 in the United Kingdom, and 21 in the United States) can lead to serious consequences. Police on campus are legally allowed to check you for alcohol if you are under age, using breathalyzers, and if you have been drinking, it could lead to detention by the police, fines, community service, or even being suspended from university. The penalties are especially bad if you are found under age, drunk on campus, so make sure that if you do choose to partake, you stay away from law enforcement.

Check Alcoholics Anonymous for help (www.alcoholics-anonymous.org.uk and www.aa.org).

And this is what our friends at realuni.com have to say about drugs:

Right, for a start let's skip the debate about the dangers of cutting pure drugs with other household goodies like talcum powder and get straight to the law bit.

The point is, drugs are illegal. End of discussion.

Anyway, if you're going to start (or keep) using, it's in your best interests to know what you're dealing with (aside from the small matter of the law). Check out these following sites, because they know what they're talking about. Also pick up all those little booklets from your doctor's surgery next time you're there. And actually read them.

Like everything else, you're old enough to make your own decisions now. Just make sure you know the risks: and don't be fooled, drugs screw up lives big time.

Check these out:

www.nida.nih.gov – (NIDA) The National Institute on Drug Abuse.

www.drugscope-dworld.org.uk – the youth section of Drugscope's website.

11

Managing your stuff

Put a little forethought into how you manage your things (clothes, toys, electronic kit, etc.) and you'll find you save lots of time and, probably, money too. Here are some pointers to help you.

11.1 Going shopping

Some students are expert shoppers long before they arrive at university; others may avoid shopping like the plague. This is for the latter camp. When you go shopping, think in advance what you want to buy and write a list if it'll help to keep you focused. Take some carrier bags with you as, increasingly, shops – particularly supermarkets – are reluctant (for good environmental reasons) to give you a new shopping bag to put your goods in. Don't forget to take your cash and debit/credit card with you too.

It often pays to look around for the best-value items. You may be able to find what you want in a second-hand or charity shop or you may find it is cheaper online. EBay and other online auction sites are, of course, also good places to look for bargains. However, when you are looking for bargains, ask yourself this: are you buying the item because it is a good price or because you really need it? Stores like to get you to buy things that you don't need, like offering cheaper prices for buying three or more items when you really only wanted one.

If you're a shopping junkie you'll probably already know how to shop successfully, but if you are managing on a much tighter budget than you've been used to, you may find you need to watch how much money your shopping habit is consuming. In particular, if you do go shopping for therapeutic reasons, be careful: you don't want to cheer yourself up with a bit of retail therapy, only to find you've got a new problem in the shape of too little money or too much debt!

11.2 Managing your electronic gizmos

- Remember to keep your gadgets' batteries charged.
- Remember to switch your phone on regularly.
- Remember to put your phone on 'silent' ring when you are in lectures or seminars.

- Keep a record of the serial numbers and makes of your electronic gadgets so that you can reclaim them if they are stolen and subsequently recovered.

- You might want to take out a repair contract for your laptop/computer so that you can get repairs done while you are at university.

- Remember to back up your work frequently.

- Make sure your electronic equipment is insured.

- Don't leave your electronic stuff lying about in obvious (thievable) places.

- Remember to take all the leads, modem lines, plugs/converters and other accessories that you need to support your gadgets.

- Try not to lose your electronic equipment.

11.3 Managing your clothes

It'll seem like a lot of work and planning, but I urge you to try to manage your clothes because you may find it actually makes your life easier.

Clothes apartheid

It may seem harsh to say it, but your clothes are happiest when they are segregated from each other. Keep your underwear separately from your skirts, dresses or trousers and both separate from your tops. That way you'll find what you're looking for much more easily than when they're all scrumpled up together.

Clean clothes

Don't wear dirty or soiled clothes if you can avoid it. Start each day with clean clothes. At the end of the day, as you take your clothes off, look at them carefully and see if there are stains or marks that need to be washed off. Sniff your clothes. If they are beginning to pong, they need to be washed! Put them in a laundry bag if you are going to do a machine load within the next week. Otherwise, you may want to handwash small items individually. See Chapter 12 below for advice on washing clothes.

Clothes maketh the (wo)man

Give some thought to what you wear. You may feel comfortable in the same clothes day in, day out, but other people have to look at you, sit with you and generally be with you and they won't like it if you look a real mess or smell or look dreadfully dishevelled. Take care with your appearance as a courtesy to others.

Conversely, if you're the kind of person who thinks you need a new outfit for every occasion, relax and save some money: most students are impoverished so they won't expect fellow-students to be modelling a new and different outfit for every occasion.

12

Cleanliness is next to Godliness

12.1 Housework

Please resist the temptation to skip this section! The regrettable truth is that housework doesn't do itself, so someone has to do it. It is, of course, possible not to do any housework ever, but if you are living in rented accommodation and/or with other people, you'll find the 'Do No Housework' option isn't, in fact, an option – unless you don't mind being evicted and/ or making enemies of your housemates. So, assuming you are going to do some housework, what's the minimum you can do without becoming a public health risk?

You may be blessed with some centrally provided cleaning service, e.g. provided by the university hall of residence, so you may find the cleaners will do some of the activities listed below. However, the cleaning services usually come with restrictions. For instance, they may clean your counter tops in the kitchen, but only if the counter tops are free of dishes and debris, so someone has to clear everything off the counter tops before the cleaners come. Knowing what the cleaners will and will not do is important, so that you can make the most of their help.

You may want to agree with your housemates which tasks are to be done by whom. You might, for example, agree to a kitchen cleaning rota or a schedule for Who Puts the Rubbish Out. It can sometimes feel a lot less arduous if the housework is shared amongst you. Agreeing on a standard of decent living at the beginning of the year is important; that way everyone knows what's being expected of them. You may be surprised at the number of students who have never cleaned anything for themselves and are alarmed when the dishes don't do themselves.

Sadly, it is quite likely that someone in your house or flat won't do their share of the housework. Don't let that someone be you. Shirking work so others have to do it or live in the pigsty you create is unacceptable. It should not be – and probably won't be – tolerated by the others in the accommodation.

Table 12.1 gives a list of housework tasks you need to do.

Table 12.1 Housework tasks

Room	Task	Frequency
Bedroom	Make bed	Every morning
	Change bedlinen	Every month
	Hoover/sweep floor	Once a week (if needed)
	Dust/wipe down surfaces	Once a month (more frequently if yukky)
	Take out used crockery and cutlery	Every day
	Tidy away clothes	Once a week
	Tidy up generally	Once a week
	Water plants	As needed or once a week
	Empty litterbin	As needed or once a week
Kitchen	Wash up	After every meal
	Put away washed things	After each wash-up
	Tidy things into cupboards	Daily
	Wipe down worksurfaces	Daily
	Wipe down sink and stove	As needed or once a week
	Wash/sweep floor	At least once a week
	Clean fridge	Once a month
	Empty wastebin	At least once a week
Bathroom	Wipe down shower/sink/bath	After use
	Take hair out of sink/shower/bath plugholes	When required
	Clean toilet	At least once a week
	Wash floor	At least once a week
	Clear out debris	A least once a week

Common areas	Remove litter	At least weekly
	Hoover/sweep floor	Once a month or as needed

The following is a list of the equipment you'll need if you are going to be doing your own housework:

J-cloths (cleaning rags) or equivalent for wiping surfaces, mopping up spills, etc.

dustpan and brush (which may be provided by the university)

broom for sweeping floors

vacuum cleaner (if you have any carpets)

mop and pail (if you have wooden, vinyl-covered or tiled floors)

duster (if you're very enthusiastic)

washing-up bowl and/or sink plug

washing-up plastic scrubbing pads and/or washing-up brush

cleaning fluids: bleach (good for cleaning sinks, loos, etc.); floor-cleaning fluid; Duck or equivalent for freshening up loos; cream cleaner for cleaning sinks, bathrooms, worksurfaces, etc.; polish (if you're keen); washing-up liquid.

Not everyone will have the same ideas about washing-up. Some people will do their dishes immediately following a meal; others will wait as long as possible. If there are simple rules, such as 'dishes must be done within 24 hours of use', it can help smooth things. Also, don't get too angry when someone doesn't do something. Do it yourself if you can't live with it not being done, and then either talk to them about it (calmly) or write them a note (the refrigerator is a good place to leave notes). In my kitchen at university, we used dry erase pens on the fridge to leave anonymous messages about things with which we were unhappy. This meant that the guilty never felt attacked and there were no ugly confrontations. For instance, the fridge might say 'someone got the stove/cooker all covered in pasta sauce, please clean it up' and usually within an hour or two the guilty would sneak in, ashamed, and deal with it, then erase the note. It was a very efficient system, and no one was ever mad at each other over the state of the kitchen.

12.2 Laundry

The following amusing and accurate description of the joys of clothes washing comes from the realuni website:

> I admit it: as an only child I was spoilt and rarely did my own washing and ironing save for dire

emergency. For this reason, I found it quite hard to do when I got to university.

I don't reckon I'm alone. I think that chances are, 80 per cent of blokes who go to university won't know how to work a washing machine properly when they get there. Nor will they know how to iron. Use this guide to gain the respect of ladies, or at least keep your clothes clean and the right colour....

12.2.1 What you need
To wash clothes, there are several items needed:

1. dirty clothes
2. washing powder
3. a washing machine, or a sink
4. preferably a drier (tumble not hair).

12.2.2 The nightmare
By the time you need to wash your clothes, you should have done with Freshers' Week and be nicely settled into your new halls.

Be prepared for washing to be a nightmare experience, with several hours wasted, and many trips up and down the stairs to the laundry.

Also be prepared for the experience to be expensive, up to £3 or $3 per load. It is important to find out how much the process will cost, and be sure to have the correct change when you decide to attack.

12.2.3 Types of washing powder
Bring some washing powder to university with you. The better the brand, the cleaner your clothes will be. Normally you will continue to use what you have had at home. This is

easiest, and clothes can feel different after being washed with different brands (bad for those of us with sensitive skin).

The choice of powder is: normal, stuff for whites and stuff for colours. Either get normal or coloured, as then you can use this for whites as well – most students will only have one type of washing powder, because it's expensive.

If you're going to get another type of powder for your whites, make sure you don't wash your colours with it!

It's best to get tablets, as powder just spills everywhere, you have to carry the whole box to the laundry, and you never know whether you have put in the correct amount.

Be careful when you buy washing powder, as there are a few things you need to know:

1. The stuff that contains bleach is for whites. Don't use it for colours.

2. Biological washing powder has enzymes in it which supposedly help the cleaning process but may not be too good for the environment.

3. Be wary of all the different fancy names.

12.2.4 How to wash your clothes

1. Take clothes to washing machine, and insert.

2. Don't overload the machine. Leave a small bit of room at the top, so that the clothes have room to move about to get clean.

3. If you're using tablet-form washing powder, take two tablets and put in stringy bag provided and wedge in with the clothes at the back of the drum.

4. If using normal powder, open drawer and pour it into the bigger of the dishes (the small one is for pre-washes by the way; more of that later).

5. Shut the door, and if necessary, insert coins.

Now comes the hard bit...picking the cycle.

Things called pre-washes are extra bits on the start that pre-wash the clothes before the main cycle. Surprising, eh? You can add extra powder if you want into the small tray – good for sports kit that is muddy, but otherwise don't bother.

12.2.5 What temperature are you going to operate at?

It used to be:

40°C/Warm – best for colours

60°C/Hot – best for whites, also for colours like socks and old clothes

but nowadays many of the washing powders are designed to be used at much lower temperatures (to save energy). You can probably do all your washes at 30°C/Cold.

The higher the temperature, the more chance there is that the clothes will shrink and/or will fade. If you're not sure, it's best to stick to 30°C/Cold. Remember it's likely that the hotter the wash, the longer the cycle will take. The bog standard cycle is Cottons at 30°C/Cold or 40°C/Warm. In our experience this is the safest to use, as washing machines are unpredictable beasts....

We have no idea how to wash things like silk as none of us has clothes made of this. Right, so that's it. Press the start button then leave.

12.2.6 Problems

First problem

You come back an hour later to find your washing had finished but that someone else wanted the machine. That someone else has put your clothes on top of the machine (because there is nowhere else to put it) from where it has fallen down the back into the manky stuff and is now more dirty than before it was washed.

Solution: Stick things back in the washing machine for a rinse and make sure you are there when they are done.

Second problem

You come back an hour later to find your washing nicely piled on top of the machine, except your Evisu jeans that cost £150 a pair. Someone has wanted the machine, but also your jeans. The problem is that there isn't a security camera, and there have been 50 people in the laundry in the last half hour.

Stealing from student laundries is a huge problem and, in general, the university will say you use the facilities at your own risk and that they will not be held liable for any loss to your property.

People can be that nasty and that weird. The number of boxer shorts I have lost is baffling (they are quite expensive). Some people must have some strange fetishes.

Solution: Work out how long the machine takes so that you know when to go to the laundry to get it out. Try to arrive a few minutes before the end of the cycle so that you don't leave your stuff unattended. The other option is to take a book or your notes and just sit in the laundry. Most places have some seating, and it can be quite nice because it is warm and smells nice, plus it seriously reduces the chance of theft.

Third problem

You have come back to put your clothes in the drier and you realize that every white shirt you own is now a slightly purple colour.

Solution: You probably did not do a very good job at sorting, and something dark got in with your whites. Find it and remove it (in my case it was a dark blue face cloth). Then put all the whites back in the washer, and select a cold rinse cycle. This will take most of the dye out. You can repeat the cold rinse cycle once more if necessary. Then pull your clothes out and hang-dry them in your room. As long as you do not wash the clothes on hot or tumble-dry them, the purple (or pink or whatever colour they ended up) will fade in time. You could also dry them, and just accept that they will be slightly coloured forever (this is how I ended up with lavender bed sheets).

12.2.7 Drying

Normally you will be provided with tumble driers. Hanging clothes in your room will take ages and will make your room smell, so use the drier unless the clothes label says not to. The symbol you need to look out for is a circle with a cross through it. This means 'Don't tumble – hang!' Put your clothes in the drier and turn it on. You will have to work out the cycle depending on what clothes you have. The hotter it is, the less time it takes to dry, but the more likely it is to shrink.

Stuff probably goes missing from driers more than machines as you can stop the drier and open the door at any time. If you have expensive clothes, it's best to take a book and an iPod, and sit there to keep an eye on it.

Quicker drying times: separate clothes into the same type for quicker drying. The thinner the clothes are, the quicker they will dry. Put t-shirts together with other thin clothes, i.e. underwear and socks and bed sheets, and put jeans, towels, etc. in a separate machine if you can.

Clean the fluff filter in the drier before you use it: this will prevent your black clothes getting covered in red fluff, and will dry your clothes more quickly, as it improves air and heat flow through the machine.

Example times: washing machines normally take around 40–60 mins. Driers normally take 30–60 mins depending on what you put in them.

12.2.8 The sink bit...

If you have one t-shirt you need to wash for going out, put a bit of washing powder in a sink with water and wash your stuff in there, then put it in the drier.

Use hot water (as hot as you can stand) and get the water frothy. Put the items in and rinse them around, in a sort of rubbing and squeezing action. Watch maternal figure for guidance. Take the items out, drain away the dirty, soapy water and put in fresh water (hot or cold, doesn't matter). Put items back in and repeat swishing about, rubbing, squeezing actions until the detergent has come out of the clothes. Take items out and hand-squeeze them to get the excess water out. Put in drier – a single t-shirt should dry in about ten minutes.

Washing more than a few items of clothing in a sink will take ages. You can't wash things like jeans or underclothes properly in a sink.

12.2.9 Ironing

This is well hard, but the more you do it, the better you get. To avoid it, take clothes out of the drier very slightly damp, and hang up on coat hangers. This way the weight of the clothes removes the creases. Clever, huh?

Do the ironing ASAP after washing; otherwise the creases become really hard to remove.

Learn the proper technique before you come to university; otherwise you will always be doomed to failure.

Note to blokes: doing the ironing in the presence of a female will make you strangely more attractive. Score unbelievable numbers of brownie points by offering to do theirs for them (only do this if you're good enough) and don't blow it by ruining their clothes.

12.3 Personal hygiene

I cannot stress strongly enough how important personal hygiene is. You *must* pay attention to this. It is not optional! You will put people off you big time if you smell, have dirty teeth, or dirty unwashed hair. If you're male, don't be badly shaven; a fuzz-free lower half of the face is best or a nice moustache (if you must) or a tidy beard is fine. Here's what you have to do:

Every morning as soon as you get up:

- shower and wash hair (can do hair washing just twice a week if you prefer)
- clean your teeth (or, if you remember to do it, you can come back after breakfast to do your teeth) and use mouthwash, if you like
- comb or brush your hair
- put deodrant under your arms
- shave if you are a man.

Go through the above routine when you are getting ready to go out in the evening too.

Shower after sports or other vigorous activity.

Always wash your hands after using the toilet.

Make sure you are wearing fresh, clean clothes. Pay particular attention to your underwear. Never wear soiled undies. (Well, you wouldn't, would you? It'd be disgusting.)

That's it, really. Easy to do and your minimal contribution to mankind.

13

Living accommodation

You need somewhere to live at university. In the first year you will probably be in university accommodation (dorms in the US). In later years you'll probably be in university-provided or private rented accommodation. Every university has an Accommodation Service with people dedicated to the task of helping you get your accommodation sorted out; use their help.

13.1 Choosing your accommodation

In the first year you will probably be able to apply for accommodation in the university's halls of residence. Make sure you follow the procedure for applying and don't miss any deadlines. Usually the application procedure is online. In second and later years you may also be able to apply for accommodation through the university's Accommodation Service. It is often the easiest way to secure suitable accommodation. Private landlords will also offer accommodation. Many local councils now run an accreditation scheme in which they register the landlord and his/her properties in an accreditation scheme which confirms that the accommodation reaches a minimum standard.

13.2 Halls of residence

Living in halls of residence (dorms in the US) is part of the ritual of university. It is usually a great deal of fun and you may find some of your lifelong friends are people with whom you shared halls/dorms. Be considerate to your fellow residents and follow the halls rules and all will be well.

If you find you are sharing halls with someone who causes you grief, go and talk to the Accommodation Service about it. They will be able to help you and can give you general assistance and advice on all aspects of your accommodation needs.

Many Halls also have a Senior Resident (or equivalent, usually called a Resident Assistant (RA) in the US). This is someone living in the halls who is a senior student or member of staff. Their job is to maintain peace and harmony in the halls. If you have one of these people in your halls, you can use them as a sounding board for any residence-related issues you may have.

No sooner have you settled into your halls than it will be time to start looking for your next year's accommodation. It varies from university to university, but often the Accommodation Service starts the Finding Accommodation process in January for a September move-in date. Keep an eye on information on the Accommodation Service's website about timing for new accommodation searches. Once again, get involved in the process early so that you can get the best choice and make sure that you don't miss any deadlines in the process.

13.3 Renting from a private landlord

If you choose or have to rent from a private landlord, make sure that you read the rental agreement carefully and understand what is in it. Your university Accommodation Service will be able to help you ensure that the agreement you are entering into is reasonable and fair.

Make sure that you know when you are allowed to be in the accommodation. Sometimes you will be in for the full academic year; other times you may need to move out for the holidays.

If you have any concerns or disputes about your accommodation, talk it through with the Accommodation Service; they will be able to help you.

13.4 Living with others

One simple rule here: be considerate of others. That's it, really.

Keep the volume down on your music and keep your noise moderate generally. Don't leave the kitchen or bathroom in a mess after you've used them. Be friendly and smiley and your housemates will love you.

13.5 A note about room-mates

It is quite common in the US, and occasionally in the UK, for students to share rooms with one or two other people. This means that everything you do, sleeping, studying, eating, will be seen by another person, and you will have to share all your space. Although this may not sound like fun, it can turn out to be a great experience. The key is to be even more considerate than you would be of your other housemates, and make sure that at the beginning of the year you lay some general ground rules to keep everything running smoothly. Another option, especially for students with Asperger's, is to avoid having a room-mate. If you have Asperger's, and you think that having a room-mate would be too difficult, contact your school's Office of Students with Disabilities (or comparable office). They will be able to take all your needs into consideration, and if you contact them early enough, they will discuss the possibility of you getting a single room. Keep in mind, however, that in the US it is quite common for a person's room-mate to be their first friend at university, and by opting for a single room you may lose an opportunity to make a friend.

14 Getting about

As a student you are entitled to one of life's little joys: a student railcard and other discounts on transport. Take full advantage of these offers and you'll save yourself lots of money. You'll probably need a passport photo to get your railcard, so remember to take one with you when you go to the station to buy your railcard.

There are also often offers through the university to get a bus pass either free or very reduced in price, because the university supports students taking public transportation. It is very tempting, especially in the US, for students to bring a car, but in the first year it is not necessary and the parking passes are usually very expensive. Consider all the public transport options before deciding that you cannot live without your car.

If you are planning to travel some distance by rail, plane or coach, you may find that you can get a cheap fare by booking well in advance. Watch it, though, because you will need to travel on the particular train/plane/coach that you book onto; you almost certainly won't be able to change your booking once you've made it.

There are a myriad of journey planner websites which will help you plan any trip and they can help you get cheap deals, so they are well worth a look.

If you are travelling a distance, e.g. on holiday, make sure that you have travel insurance in place.

If you lose stuff when you are travelling, it is always worth asking in the transport provider's Lost Property office as the transport staff may find your lost item and put it into Lost Property for you. It can take several days for lost items to make it to a Lost Property office, so keep checking from time to time.

Be careful when you are travelling to make sure you don't get into situations where you might be vulnerable. For example, try to keep in busy areas when you're on train or bus journeys. Never accept lifts from strangers. Plan your travel so that you don't end up stranded late at night in some dodgy place.

15

Studying

You are going to university to study. That is the basic idea. Sometimes it is easy to lose sight of that basic idea when there's so much else going on. Having gone to all the effort of getting to university, don't blow it when you're there by not doing enough studying. Some courses may have very few hours a week in proper lectures and tutorials, but you will probably be expected to do a lot of work in your own time. This will take the form of research, reading and essay and project writing. Don't be fooled into thinking this is easy, because it's not. Especially when there are so many other things you could be doing that are more fun. Here are some tips to make studying easier, in addition to the studying tips and time management strategies that have already been mentioned in Chapter 3.

15.1 Planning your work

The University at Buffalo has the following to say about studying at university. It sounds rather scary – the reality isn't so bad!

> University classes are a great deal more difficult than high school classes. There are more reading assignments, and the exams and papers cover a greater amount of material. Instructors expect students to do more work outside the classroom. In order to survive, the student must take responsibility for his or her actions. This means the student needs to follow the course outlines and keep up with the readings. The student must do the initiating. If a class is missed, it is up to the student to borrow lecture notes from someone who was present. If the student is having difficulty with course work, he or she needs to ask for help – ask to do extra work, request an appointment with an academic advisor, or sign up for tutoring or other academic-skills training.

The website www.realuni.com has a rather more student-led approach. They say:

> Science courses tend to be based around lectures – which makes it easier for those of you who find it hard to be bothered to do something. Art and Design courses are the real nightmare, where individual projects can last several weeks. You start with the first introduction project briefing, and then you do what you want until the deadline, maybe

with various meetings with tutors once weekly or
so to discuss how it's going. For this kind of course
you really need self-discipline. If you're going to do
humanities, just make sure you can write essays…

It's up to you how you plan your work schedule. Just try
to use your time efficiently. There's no point spending all
evening working instead of going out when you wasted the
morning staying in bed or watching television.

Just set yourself a target, and try to stick to it. I never
needed much sleep so used to work one weekend morning
before everyone else got up, and used to do bits here and
there if I had a free morning/afternoon. It's always best to get
on with your work when no-one else is around as then there
are fewer distractions.

Obviously it's easier in winter because it gets dark earlier
and it's raining outside. Remember to try and keep up
with the work as you go along. A little bit here and there
throughout the year is much better than cramming it all in
the final term.

If you find it hard to work in your room, then try moving
to another study area, where there are no distractions!

You know how to work, and how to revise, so it's up
to you from now on. It's all about self-discipline, and how
effectively you use your time. The best policy to follow is to
make sure when you work, you work, and when you don't, go
and do something fun.

15.2 Importance of deadlines and time management

Deadlines are important in your studying. If you repeatedly
hand in work late (or not at all) or are unprepared for seminars
and tutorials, you'll end up being expelled, which would be a
shame, to put it mildly.

And remember that work takes time so don't muck about leaving your work undone until the eleventh hour and then hope to be able to get it done the night before it is due to be handed in. The chances are that you won't have left yourself enough time, with the result that not only will you put yourself under intolerable stress, but you'll make a mess of what you are trying to do. So *plan ahead* and give yourself more time than you'll actually need to get the work done. If you are a procrastinator, trick yourself by making your deadline to complete the work a day earlier than the actual deadline and work to your own deadline. Of course you won't really fool yourself, but it can be a good way of disciplining yourself.

If you find you can't cure yourself of poor time management, then have a look at Chapter 3 on time management and get a book on the subject or get help from the university support services. You are going to have a lifetime of working to deadlines (whether you like it or not), so use your time at university to teach yourself some good habits about time management.

15.3 Notes for people on the autistic spectrum

Studying at university can take a bit of getting used to, particularly if change or lack of clear structure can be problematic for you. The University of Melbourne's online guide *Towards Success in Tertiary Study with Asperger's Syndrome* has some suggestions to help you as follows.

15.3.1 Getting started

- Contact specialist support services at the university before the course begins to discuss special arrangements.
- Set up efficient, colour-coded filing systems for each subject and lists of equipment required for each class.

- Create a comprehensive timetable to map out assessment tasks (commencement and due dates) and exam dates. Academic/Study Skills Advisers can help set realistic goals and study plans.

- Establish study routines: break tasks into manageable sections; alternate interesting with less interesting tasks; avoid distractions and focus on completion.

- Organize a quiet, interruption-free study zone.

- Get course outlines and booklists before semester begins and start any reading.

- Maintain a life balance: allow time for socializing, exercise, relaxation and sleep.

15.3.2 Study techniques and tips
1. Lectures and tutorials

- Attend all lectures, tutorials and laboratory sessions, especially the first ones when most of the important information is given about the course. Find out what was covered in any sessions missed.

- Arrive early and decide where to sit: at the front to maximize concentration as there are fewer distractions; at the back next to an aisle or an exit door if breaks or movement are necessary.

- If concentration is a problem, consider attending repeat lectures and ask lecturers for copies of notes or other material. Consider recording lectures (but check with the lecturer before you do so).

- Do preparatory reading for all lectures and tutorials.

- If organizing material or writing quickly is a problem, use a laptop to take notes or explore support options.

- Do not interrupt in lectures unless students are invited to do so.

- Students are expected to participate but not dominate tutorial discussions: learn and practise cues for taking turns in conversation; find a balance between contributing and listening to others.

- Avoid behaviour that others will consider odd or rude, e.g. repeating questions/comments and speaking thoughts aloud.

- Be fully prepared for tutorial presentations: practise and time your delivery; organize notes and highlight key points; prepare questions to stimulate discussion; make eye contact with the audience.

2. Preparing assignments

- Clarify the required academic style for written assignments. Ask lecturers and Academic/Study Skills Advisers for copies of model assignments.

- Explore concept maps software such as Inspiration and Endnote to facilitate organizing ideas, planning, structure and referencing tasks.

- Prioritize tasks and reading; determine and focus on purpose of reading before beginning; record main points and bibliographic details at the same time as reading.

3. Exams

- Make arrangements early for any alternative assessments. Speak to your tutor early if you think you may need an alternative approach to an assessment.

- Select relevant material and gear revision to suit exam style. Seek explanations for anything not clearly understood.

- Explore memory enhancement techniques such as Mind Tools.
- Plan and adhere to times for each question in exams.
- Use relaxation techniques during exams.

16

Getting the most out of university

16.1 Using the facilities

Universities usually have amazing facilities for students, from fabulous laboratories and lecture theatres to brilliant dance and concert venues, excellent sports facilities, beautiful gardens and grounds, excellent transport links and so on.

What's even better is that everyone is in more or less in the same boat, so you can enjoy using the facilities without feeling foolish or awkward because you are a beginner or inexpert at what you are doing.

The best university students are those who are willing to give it a go, to try out new things and develop into new areas of interest. It is an opportunity to experiment and to try out things that may – or may not – become activities that you'll want to pursue for some time.

Sometimes the most difficult thing to do is to overcome your reticence or shyness and just give it a go. But do try, you may be pleasantly surprised by what you find!

16.2 Asking people

There are always people available to ask even your stupidest questions. The university has all sorts of advisers and counsellors on its payroll so don't hesitate to search out the ones who'll be able to give you the help you need.

The Students' Union is often a great place to start a line of enquiry as often they'll have experience of what you're enquiring about.

Some universities have a Personal Tutor system in which an academic is assigned to you as your academic and pastoral care provider. They are there to help you, so, if in doubt, talk to your Personal Tutor, if you have one.

Don't forget that your old support network – your family – may well be able to help you, too.

Expanding your horizons

17.1 Travel

One of the great things about university is the long vacations. If you can afford to do so, university vacations are a good time to do some travelling. There are excellent trips that you can make, just travelling (e.g. Explore, Trailfinders) or travelling and volunteering (try Volunteering Holidays Abroad, Volunteering Vacations, campsinternational.com, The Pod Site, Alternative Breaks, etc.). Plan your holiday well in advance so that you can get the greatest choice and the best deals.

17.2 The library (real and online)

Universities, not surprisingly, have brilliant libraries. Libraries are no longer the fuddy-duddy places of yore but now have lots of different ways of sourcing the knowledge you need. The Library staff are experts in researching information; befriend them and they'll make your study so much easier. Finding and using libraries outside your university can be a mini-adventure, and can make you feel like (and be!) a real researcher.

17.3 Diversity

Increasingly universities are becoming international places. You can have a lot of fun being with people from different cultures, learning about the way they approach life. Some of the differences in the detail are fascinating. Many campuses now have Cross-Cultural Centres, or equivalent, where you can meet international students and have group meetings about international cultural matters. It is a great resource both for those who are interested in broadening their cultural knowledge, and those who are interested in going abroad.

17.4 Volunteering

Another way to learn more about the world we live in is to get involved in volunteering. Most universities have active volunteering groups and students get a lot of enjoyment out of volunteering in their local community or further afield. Volunteering also gives you useful experience for the world of work and looks good on your CV. Yet another reason for getting involved.

17.5 Gap Year

Gap years go in and out of fashion. In the 1980s people routinely took a gap year before going to university. Currently they are less popular, but people choosing to take a gap year are now more flexible about when they take it, sometimes taking it before going to university and sometimes taking it after they've graduated.

If your course is a sandwich course or a language (or other) course in which you spend a year studying or working outside the university, you will get a sort-of gap year within your degree course. Preparing for the year you'll spend away from your home university takes a bit of work and planning. As ever, the sooner you start looking into what is available, where you can go, what you can do, etc., the better. You can get some ideas by asking students who are ahead of you on your course what they are planning to do/have done and by talking to academics and staff involved in your course.

For students in the United States, taking time off before going to university is quite rare. However, it is much more common for American students to go abroad for a year of study at a foreign university, which can be an eye-opening experience, like the gap years are for British students. Taking a year abroad is a very good way to become a better global citizen, and the change of pace affects many students for the better. Plus, it is a ton of fun.

18 The end (but it is just the beginning)

Congratulations if you've read this far!

A final word: you've done fantastically well to get to university, no one can take your achievements to date away from you. Give yourself a pat on the back for that.

As you go through university you'll have rich experiences which will be important foundations for your life ahead. Not everything will go well or just as you hoped, but put the bad bits down to experience, leave them behind, pick yourself up again and look forward to the future. If things get tough, talk to someone. There are people in the university support system who are there to help you through: use their services.

University life can be hugely enjoyable, so relax, don't worry about what others will think of you (provided you're doing your bit to be a civilized member of the human race), take a deep breath and go for it. Smile as much as you can – it'll make you and others feel happy.

And remember, back home your family and friends love you very much and are there in the background cheering for you.

ENJOY YOURSELF. GOOD LUCK!

Checklist: what to take with you to university

With thanks to www.realuni.com for most of this list.

How much to take

No doubt you've got a lot of stuff in your bedroom. How much are you going to take with you?

Remember, unless you've seen the hall you're going to move into on an open day, you won't know how big the room will be.

You can only take as much stuff as will fit in a car. A fully loaded averaged-sized car is as much as you should take. You'll also acquire a lot of stuff over the term, which can prove difficult when it comes to taking it home again!

What to take

First, you need to separate what you're going to take into two categories: what you really need and what would be nice if there was room.

Once you've filled the car with what you *have* to take, you can decide what else you would *like* to take.

What you really need

Let's start with the basics. Copy this off and use it as a checklist if you want.

Bedding
- [ ] 1 or 2 pillows
- [ ] Duvet/comforter
- [ ] Underblanket/mattress pad (between mattress and sheet)
- [ ] 2 sets of bed linen (usually extra-long twin size in the US)
- [ ] Towels
- [ ] Wash cloth
- [ ] Beach towel (if your university is near the coast)

Clothes
- [ ] Lots of them (take enough to not have to do washing often)
- [ ] Lots of socks are essential, as they go missing from laundry
- [ ] Suit jacket/dinner jacket/tuxedo/beautiful dress and nice shoes for formal dinners
- [ ] Party/clubbing wear
- [ ] Sports equipment (football gear, etc.)
- [ ] School uniform for school disco (or closest thing you have to a uniform)

Wash stuff
- [ ] Toothbrush, toothpaste, floss and mouthwash if you use it
- [ ] Soap/showergel
- [ ] All your makeup/beauty products
- [ ] Flip-flops
- [ ] Take lots of soap and get a soap dish; otherwise you'll drop it on the way to the shower and the soap will get fluffy
- [ ] Shower bag for supplies, or shower caddy
- [ ] Shampoo and conditioner
- [ ] Hairbrush and comb
- [ ] Deodorant
- [ ] Q-tips
- [ ] Sun screen
- [ ] Nail clipper/file
- [ ] Robe/dressing gown
- [ ] Razor with shaving cream

Kitchen stuff (with your name on *everything*)

☐ Many sets of cheap cutlery, as they go missing very easily
☐ 1 serving spoon
☐ 1 bottle opener and 1 can opener
☐ Containers for leftovers
☐ 2 dinner plates and 2 bowls
☐ 2 mugs
☐ 2 pint glasses
☐ 2 saucepans – 1 large and 1 medium/small
☐ 1 frying pan – preferably non-stick
☐ 1 big oven tray
☐ 1 wooden spoon for stirring
☐ 1 colander for pasta draining (don't try using the saucepan lid)
☐ 1 chopping board
☐ 1 sharp knife
☐ Tea towel/kitchen towel
☐ Oven glove
☐ Tea bags
☐ Sugar, salt and pepper
☐ Microwave popcorn
☐ Instant soup/noodles (for emergencies when you are too hungry/tired/hungover to cook)

Cleaning stuff

You absolutely will need:
☐ A sponge
☐ Washing-up liquid/dish soap
☐ Paper towels/kitchen roll
☐ A roll or two of toilet paper for when it runs out
☐ Something for scrubbing disgusting dishes (very abrasive)
☐ Some spray cleaner for surfaces

You might not need the following if you are going to be in halls of residence or in accommodation that comes with a cleaner (best) or where cleaning equipment is supplied (second best), so check what the university provides before buying this stuff:

□ J-cloths or equivalent for wiping surfaces, mopping up spills, etc.

□ Dustpan and brush

□ Broom for sweeping floors

□ Vacuum cleaner (if you have any carpets)

□ Mop and pail (if you have wooden, vinyl-covered or tiled floors)

□ Duster (if you're very enthusiastic)

□ Washing-up bowl and/or sink plug

□ Washing-up plastic scrubbing pads and/or washing-up brush

□ Cleaning fluids: bleach (good for cleaning sinks, loos, etc.); floor cleaning fluid; Duck or equivalent for freshening up loos; cream cleaner for cleaning sinks, bathrooms, worksurfaces, etc.; polish (if you're keen); washing-up liquid.

Work stuff

□ Backpack or bag of some sort

□ Folders for work

□ Plastic folders

□ Well-stocked pencil case

□ Scissors, hole punch, ruler, rubber, pencil sharpener, stapler, prit stick glue and blu-tack, pins

□ Sellotape/sticking tape, lined paper, post-it notes, index cards, paper clips

□ Plenty of biros/bic pens

□ Loads of dividers for your folders

□ Calculator, even if you're doing English

□ Notebooks

□ Any supplies that you used in school and were essential to your organizational process.

Tip: Keeping all your work organized is the secret of doing well: make sure you have a folder for each subject.

Tip: Get the folders at the start of term, and keep them organized from the start. Even if you don't do any work in the evening to start with, make sure you've got all the notes, and in the right order.

Tip: If you have loads of courses at the same time, have one folder that you take to classes with the current work in it for every subject, and one (more likely ten) bigger folder(s) at home for each subject that has all the other work in it. This way, your work will be kept neat and uncrumpled, and you won't have to carry loads of stuff to uni everyday. As the folder gets full, move some of the old stuff out and into the folders in your room. This way you only have to carry the stuff you need to university.

Electronic kit

☐ Mobile phone
☐ Mobile phone charger
☐ Laptop
☐ Laptop power supply
☐ Printer (you may not need your own but if you do, don't forget the ancillary stuff too: cables to attach printer to computer, printer cartridges, printer paper)
☐ iPod
☐ iPod earphones
☐ iPad
☐ iPAQ/BlackBerry or other personal organizer (optional)

Stuff that would be nice to have

Other electrical goods

From now on it's up to you. These things are expensive. Make sure you get insurance for them.

☐ TV – it helps fill those boring moments, not that you'll have many. It also helps to bring people into your room. You will need to buy a licence – they cost a lot of money.
☐ PlayStation/Wii – fun, but you should have better things to be doing with your time. It'll get people into your room, especially with good multiplayer games, but then you need a TV as well…
☐ Mini-fridge (common in the US because many dorms don't have kitchens). Don't bring things that aren't allowed, such as microwaves.

The rest

The rest of what you take is optional, but here's a list of things you will probably need.

☐ Alarm clock

☐ Watch

☐ Radio

☐ Desk lamp x 3 – You may need several of these as old student halls have a reputation for being quite dark. You shouldn't be paying for the electricity anyway, so who cares? Get those cheapy ones from a well-known Swedish furniture manufacturer that cost about a fiver. Check regulations about extension leads, though; you may only be allowed one.

☐ Sports equipment – you'll probably feel the need to start playing loads of sport once you get to university. Make sure you've got your football boots.

☐ Rollerblades if you've got them

☐ Frisbees are good too

☐ Washing powder

☐ Stain remover stick or spray

☐ Bin bags/garbage bags

☐ Laundry bag

☐ Sleeping bag if you've got one

☐ Posters (highly recommended for making your room feel like your own), but check regulations about putting things on walls.

☐ First Aid kit – plasters/band-aids, aspirin, antiseptic cream, cotton wool, cough drops, vitamins, lip balm, thermometer, enough pain relievers to help you through a few hangovers

☐ Tin foil – use it to cover grill pans before putting food, etc. on. This way the foil catches all the oil, and you don't have to wash the pan up. Sorted!

☐ Umbrella (really not optional – you will get rained on eventually, no matter where you are at university)

☐ Camera – record your freshers' week 'cos it will be wicked!

☐ Condoms (also not that optional)

☐ Clothes hangers

☐ Clothes pegs

☐ Storage boxes

☐ Kettle (may be provided by the university).

Budget planner

INCOME	£ / $	EXPENDITURE	£ / $
Tuition fee loan		Tuition fee	
Maintenance loan		Rent	
Parental contribution		Utility bills (gas, electricity, water)	
Maintenance grant/ special support grant		Food (eating in and out)	
Any additional grants or allowances		Travel costs (public transport during term time and to and from home)	
Savings		Study costs (books, course materials, photocopying, library costs, etc.)	
Earnings from part-time work during term time		Mobile phone and internet	
Earnings during vacations		Insurance (contents and possessions)	
Bank overdraft		Socializing	
		Toiletries	

INCOME	£/$	EXPENDITURE	£/$
		Laundry	
		Clothes and shoes	
		Home entertainment (DVDs, CDs, etc.) and presents	
		Sports and leisure	
		Costs during the vacations	
		Special costs, e.g. travel (and travel insurance), field trip, etc.	
		Emergencies	
TOTAL INCOME		**TOTAL EXPENDITURE**	
Surplus/shortfall			

Useful websites

Below are some links to some decent websites that are useful and relevant to this book.

Alcohol

Alcoholics Anonymous – 0845 7697555 – www.alcoholics-anonymous.org.uk

Alcohol Concern – www.alcoholconcern.org.uk

National Institute on Alcohol Abuse and Alcoholism (NIAAA) – www.niaaa.nih.gov

Drugs

Hit – www.hit.org.uk

The National Institute on Drug Abuse (NIDA) – www.nida.nih.gov

Drugscope – www.drugscope.org.uk

National Drugs Helpline (UK) – 0800 776600 – www.urban75.com/Drugs/helpline.html

National Hotline for Drug Treatment (US) – 1-800-662-4357

Finances

www.nusonline.co.uk

Gap year links

i-to-i – www.i-to-i.com – i-to-i is an international organization specializing in volunteer and teaching placements.

www.gap-year.com

www.yearoutgroup.org

www.gapwork.com

Health links

NetDoctor – www.netdoctor.co.uk

Samaritans – www.samaritans.org.uk

Job links

www.volunteerafrica.org

Meningitis

Meningitis Trust – www.meningitis-trust.org.uk

Open days

OpenDays.com – www.opendays.com

Safe sex

The Terrence Higgins Trust – www.tht.co.uk

Useful stuff

UCAS – www.ucas.com

NUS Online – www.nusonline.co.uk

Push – www.push.co.uk

The Autistic Self-Advocacy Network – www.autisticadvocacy.org

References

Alcoholics Anonymous. (The AA Portal). Available at www.alcoholics-anonymous.org.uk.

Alcoholics Anonymous. 'Welcome to Alcoholics Anonymous'. Available at www.aa.org.

All About Students. 'All About Students – Home'. Available at www.allaboutstudents.co.uk/.

Al-Mahmood, Reem, McLean, Patricia, Powell, Elizabeth and Ryan, Janette. *Towards Success in Tertiary Study*, University of Melbourne. Available at www.services.unimelb.edu.au/edp/downloads/aspergers.pdf.

Attwood, Sarah. (2008) *Making Sense of Sex: A Forthright Guide to Puberty, Sex and Relationships for People with Asperger's Syndrome*. London: Jessica Kingsley Publishers.

British Broadcasting Company. 'Emotional Health – Anger Management'. Available at www.bbc.co.uk/health/emotional_health/mental_health/coping_angermanagement.shtml.

British Broadcasting Company. 'Health'. BBC Home. Available at www.bbc.co.uk/health.

British Broadcasting Company. 'The Surgery – Health'. BBC Home. Available at www.bbc.co.uk/switch/surgery/advice, www.bbc.co.uk/radio1/onelife/health.

Camps International. 'Camps International – Home'. Available at www.campsinternational.com.

Carnegie, Dale. *How to Win Friends and Influence People*. New York: Pocket Books, 1936.

Center for Disease Control. 'Sexual Health'. Available at www.cdc.gov/sexualhealth.

Center for Disease Control. 'Exercise for Adults' CDC Website, redirect from Health and Human Services Website. www.cdc.gov/physicalactivity/everyone/guidelines/adults.html.

Citizens Advice Bureau. 'Citizens Advice Bureau – Home'. Available at www. citizensadvice.co.uk.

Department of Economics and Finance. 'Department of Economics and Finance – Home'. Durham University. Available at www.dur.ac.uk/economics. finance.

Depression Alliance. 'Depression Alliance – Help and Information about Depression Symptoms'. Available at www.depressionalliance.org.

Drug Scope. 'Welcome to Drug Scope'. Available at www.drugscope.org.uk.

E4S. 'Student Jobs, Internships, and Graduate Jobs'. Available at www.e4s.co.uk.

Edberg, Henrik. *The Positivity Blog*. Available at www.positivityblog.com.

Elliot, Roger. 'Improve Self-Confidence and Self-esteem' Uncommon Knowledge. Available at www.self-confidence.co.uk.

Federal Trade Commission. 'Facts for Consumers'. Available at www.ftc.gov/ bcp/edu/pubs/consumer/credit/cre13.shtm.

Financial Services Authority. 'FSA – Home'. Available at www.fsa.gov.uk.

Financial Services Authority. 'Money Made Clear – Loans Made Clear'. Available at www.moneymadeclear.org.uk/products/loans/loans.html.

Financial Services Authority. 'Money Made Clear – Savings'. Available at www. moneymadeclear.org.uk/hubs/home_savings.html.

HM Revenue and Customs. 'HM Revenue and Customs – Students FAQ'. Available at www.hmrc.gov.uk/students/faqs.htm.

Internal Revenue Service. 'IRS – Home'. Available at www.irs.gov.

Mind Tools. 'Physical Relaxation Techniques'. Available at www.mindtools.com/ pages/article/newTCS_05.htm.

Morris, Desmond. (1978) *Manwatching: A Field Guide to Human Behaviour.* Triad Books.

National Debt Line. 'Free Confidential Advice'. Available at www. nationaldebtline.co.uk.

National Institute of Health. 'The Science of Drug Abuse and Addiction – Students and Young Adults'. The National Institute on Drug Abuse. Available at www.nida.nih.gov.

National Health Services. 'Playing It Safe', Sexual Health. Available at www. sexualhealth.org.uk.

NetDoctor. 'Health and Well-being'. Available at www.netdoctor.co.uk.

NetDoctor. 'Self-esteem'. Available at www.netdoctor.co.uk/sex_relationships/ facts/selfesteem.htm.

The RealUni Alternative University Guide. 'Alternative Prospectus', RealUni. Available at www.realuni.com.

Royal College of Psychiatrists. 'Cognitive Behavioral Therapy'. Available at www.rcpsych.ac.uk/mentalhealthinfoforall/treatments/cbt.aspx.

Segar, Mark. *Coping: A Survival Guide for People with Asperger Syndrome* The University of York. Available at www-users.cs.york.ac.uk/~alistair/survival. This is also available as a hard copy book from the Early Years Diagnostic Centre, run by the charity Nottingham Regional Society for Autistic Children and Adults (NORSACA), tel: +44 (0) 1623 490879.

Stanford University. 'Environmental Health & Safety'. Available at www.stanford. edu/dept/EHS/prod/general/ergo/keys.html.

Student Jobs. 'Find Your Next Student Job'. Available at www.student-jobs.co.uk.

Student Recipes. 'Student Recipes – Home'. Available at www.studentrecipes. com.

The Complete University Guide. 'The Complete University Guide – Home'. Available at www.thecompleteuniversityguide.co.uk/single.htm?ipg=6605.

The Terrence Higgins Trust. 'Home – Talking About Sex'. Available at www.tht. org.uk.

The Learning Center Academic Skills Resources. 'Time Management'. The University of New South Wales. Available at www.lc.unsw.edu.au/onlib/ time3.html.

The Student Room. 'Student Food'. Available at www.thestudentroom.co.uk/ wiki/Student_Food.

UCAS. 'How to Manage your Money'. Available at www.ucas.ac.uk/students/ startinguni/managing_money/budgeting.

United States Financial Literacy and Education Commission. 'My Money – Home'. My Money website. Available at www.mymoney.gov.

University at Buffalo Counseling Services. 'Tips for Adjusting to University Life'. Available at www.ub-counseling.buffalo.edu/adjusting.shtml.

University of Southampton Students Union. *University of Southampton Students Union Handbook.* 2009.

US Department of Health and Human Services. 'Exercise and fitness'. Available at www. hhs.gov/safety/index.html.

USA Jobs. 'Student Jobs'. Available at www.usajobs.gov/studentjobs.

WebMD. 'Better Information, Better Health'. Available at www.webmd.com.

Index